MARRIAGEABILITY

MARRIAGEABILITY

*Embracing the Richness of a Marriage
Affected by Disability*

JOAN M. BORTON

MarriageAbility
Copyright © 2023 by Joan M. Borton
All rights reserved.

Published in the United States of America by Credo House Publishers, a division of Credo Communications LLC, Grand Rapids, Michigan
credohousepublishers.com

ISBN: 978-1-62586-256-3

Unless otherwise indicated, Scripture quotations are taken from the Holy Bible, New International Version®, NIV®. Copyright © 1973, 1978, 1984, 2011 by Biblica, Inc.™ Used by permission of Zondervan. All rights reserved.

Cover and interior design by Frank Gutbrod
Editing by Donna Huisjen

Printed in the United States of America
First edition

To my Junior Shepherd, Jerry Lee Borton,
who loves me and cares for me
while heartily following the Senior Shepherd,
our Lord Jesus Christ

CONTENTS

Foreword 1
Introduction 5

SECTION ONE ELEMENTS OF A BIBLICAL MARRIAGE

Chapter One: *Becoming One* 11
Chapter Two: *Submit or Die* 19
Chapter Three: *Vows and Dreams* 31
Chapter Four: *Intimacy* 45

SECTION TWO THE DAILINESS OF DISABILITY

Chapter Five: *Adjustments* 59
Chapter Six: *Typical Spouse Roles* 71
Chapter Seven: *The Caregiving Spouse* 79
Chapter Eight: *Home and Family* 91
Chapter Nine: *Attendant Care* 103
Chapter Ten: *Travel* 115
Chapter Eleven: *Make Room for Fun* 129
Chapter Twelve: *Aging* 143

SECTION THREE LIFE IN COMMUNITY
Chapter Thirteen: *Hard Truths* 157
Chapter Fourteen: *Is Marriage for Me?* 167

Appendix 185
Cincinnati Chili Recipe 185
Buckeye Recipe 186
Resources 189
Acknowledgments 191
Endnotes 195

FOREWORD

I'm glad you picked up this book. My prayer is that it both encourages and challenges you.

I can assure you that the author knows a few things about marriage and disability. I've been her husband for almost twenty-eight years. Over the years God continues to mold us into his image and make us one.

Along with the joys and challenges of marriage, we live with the everyday realities of my disability. I was born with cerebral palsy (CP) and use a power wheelchair. Every person with cerebral palsy is different. For me, it means that the part of my brain that controls my balance and coordination is damaged. This means that the messages don't get through correctly from my brain to the rest of my body. I know this is an oversimplified definition, but this is a book on marriage and disability, not a science textbook.

Joan and I got married in our mid-thirties. At the time, each of us was coming to terms with the idea that we might never marry. For me, dating was difficult. Sometimes years went by between dates. I would try too hard. I expected too much. I poured all my energy into ministry.

I'd met Joan seven years earlier at a disability ministry conference in Wisconsin. There were forty-eight people there. She remembers me because she said I was funny and wore polyester. In my defense, polyester is easier for transfers. I don't remember meeting her. I'm pretty sure she has forgiven me by now. Thank you, Jesus, . . . and Joan.

We met again the next year at a conference in Michigan. There were over nine hundred people there. It was there that I remember meeting her. We were part of a group that hung out together between sessions. We kept meeting at the same conference for several years. Besides hanging out, she would accompany me to the local pharmacy to pick up the prescription I had forgotten to bring with me. At least once, she even paid for it. Somehow, she still understood that I'm a competent adult.

We had fun together from the moment I remembered meeting her. We still do.

Clearly, I married up. I married my best friend. Joan is a picture of God's grace to me. Nobody knows my baggage better than she does . . . except Jesus. And they both still love me.

As you read, I hope you'll laugh at many of our stories—as we do. If you wonder if the stories are real, they are. And yes, I encouraged Joan to tell these stories with my blessing, even the ones about me. But after you shake your head and laugh, I hope you'll look again at the truth behind the story.

Joan is my primary caregiver. Growing up with a disability, I learned to be independent. But I'm faster when I have someone to help me physically. Some of our friends who also live with disabilities in the family say that the spouse should never be the caregiver. For others like us, it works. Caregiving in marriage is a personal decision.

No one will care for me in quite the same way, or as well, as Joan does. She assists me with getting up in the morning and going to bed at night and lots of other tasks in between. Sometimes she's my physical therapist, advocate, chauffeur, . . . and the list goes on. No wonder she found it difficult to carve out time to write.

We still talk about hiring attendants. And I continue to drag my feet (funny how I can do that when they sit on the footrests of my wheelchair). There's a day coming soon when we will use attendants. But, I repeat, no one will care for me in quite the same way, or as well, as Joan does.

We also do ministry together. To learn more about our work, please visit Luke14Echange.org.

We've learned to be intentional about dating and keeping our marriage strong. There are seasons when we do better with this than others. Joan and I know keenly that our marriage is still a work in progress. We're blessed that we share a lot of laughter—and an occasional tear along the way.

Early readers suggested that this book would be helpful for any marriage. That may be true. But Joan wrote this book with you in mind—for couples whose marriage includes disability. You are our tribe.

Enjoy.

Jerry Borton

INTRODUCTION

We were four years into marriage when we met Frank and Julia Burnett. They were members of a church we visited.

Then in their twenty-third year of marriage, challenges overwhelmed them. While engaged, they had dreamed of serving together in full-time church ministry after he graduated from Bible college. Those hopes vanished just six weeks after their wedding. Frank was in a horrendous auto accident that left him with seizures, a brain injury, and multiple physical disabilities. Julia was his sole caregiver.

Now, after we had visited the church again, Julia invited us to come to their home the following Sunday for lunch. Over store-bought chicken salad sandwiches, potato salad, and coleslaw, they told us, "You're the first couple we've met who live with disability in your marriage."

What? They had already been married five times longer than we had. How could they never have met another couple like them?

Though they felt accepted and loved by their fellow church members, Julia and Frank also felt isolated and misunderstood.

That afternoon the loneliness and pain of twenty-three years tumbled out.

I wrote this book because of the Burnetts. I never want to hear of another couple who lives with disability in their marriage and knows no one else like themselves. We all need role models and mentors. Jerry and I are not perfect. And we certainly don't have all the answers. We may never meet you in person, but it is our hope that, by reading parts of our story, you may feel less alone.

There are three sections to this book. Section One details my understanding of what the Bible says about marriage. These principles are no different for couples with disabilities than for others. But I believe that these elements build the foundation for all that follows.

Section Two deals with many of the day-to-day scenarios disability throws our way. The manner in which Jerry and I address these may vary from the approach you and your spouse take. That's great. I share our stories and some questions we've pondered to kick-start your thinking, not to imply that they are the right or only way.

I wrote Section Three for the surrounding community. Chapter Thirteen seeks to create understanding for those who don't live with disability but know someone who does. The final chapter is for singles who wonder, because of their disability, whether they will ever get married.

Each chapter ends with two sets of *Embracing* points (variously worded). The first set is for the couple living with a disability in their marriage. These questions facilitate conversation between you and your spouse. The second set, *Embracing Your Friends,* is for the nondisabled reader who wants to know how to support their friends with disability.

If you need counseling and help with your marriage on a deeper level, please reach out to a pastor or therapist in your community. If you have trouble locating one, please reach out to me, and I will network to help you find one.

I pray for blessings on your marriage as you forge ahead to embrace the richness of a marriage affected by disability.

SECTION ONE

ELEMENTS OF A BIBLICAL MARRIAGE

ONE
BECOMING ONE

Two equals one? Although the modern education system uses a new system to explain math, the concept of two equals one seems counterintuitive. But in Matthew 19:4–6, the Bible says,

"'Haven't you read,' [Jesus] replied, 'that at the beginning the Creator "made them male and female," and said, "For this reason a man will leave his father and mother and be united to his wife, and the two will become one flesh"? So they are no longer two, but one flesh. Therefore what God has joined together, let no one separate.'"

Couples often incorporate visual symbols into their wedding ceremony. Two popular ones are the lighting of a unity candle and the pouring of colored sand to represent the merging of their lives. These symbols offer some understanding, though the actual process of two people becoming one is more challenging and time-consuming than can be implied by a simple gesture. Genuine oneness begins with emotional and spiritual unity. It requires a conscious choice from each person to set aside their own agenda and preferences for the sake of the other. Spiritual agreement involves the mystery of yielding control and authority to God.

Becoming one is a journey, a lifelong process. Even with almost three decades of marriage behind us, there are moments when Jerry and I still gaze at each other and wonder, W*here did you come from? Do you truly know me?*

Jordan Sok, a young married man, wrote, "I mean that just like metal . . . being melted to fit with another metal, marriage breaks down areas of your life that have never been broken down before. And that process is painful."[1]

But within this relinquishment lies a beautiful revelation. Becoming one with my husband means that his challenges are mine, and mine have become his. We share not only the burdens, but also the joys of life. Neither of us has to face a situation alone. What one of us does affects the other. Our lives are interdependent. Jerry often says, "I can't believe that, other than God, Joan is the only person who knows my stuff and still loves me."

Being one doesn't imply a lack of disagreement, enjoyment of the same activities, or identical thought processes. In fact, as I write this, we find ourselves in a humorous miscommunication. While I'm at the public library, Jerry is in his home office. Our attempts to communicate via text and email have failed to convey our intended messages. Frustrated, I finally gave up and called him. If only oneness included mind meld.

When two become one, life can no longer be solely about oneself. However, this doesn't mean that we are to ignore personal development or make our spouse responsible for everything. I no longer live, think, or act solely on the basis of *my* desires. Instead, our operating system revolves around considering each other's needs and desires. Becoming one is a *we* endeavor.

At the time of our first anniversary, we attended a marriage conference called Family Life Weekend to Remember. One exercise the speaker led involved facing our spouses and declaring, "We are Jerry and Joan Borton, another one of God's great ideas." Although this may sound amusing, the statement holds truth. We periodically remind ourselves of this and often open sessions we teach on marriage with this affirmation.

We celebrate our unique gifts, skills, and talents and look for opportunities to use them, perhaps together. Blending our strengths creates a united purpose for our days, our energy, and our focus. Together, our aim is to bring glory to God, to love one another, and to encourage individuals and families affected by disability.

Prayer is one way to grow in oneness. I hear my husband's heart when we pray together. I cherish the time we sit face-to-face or side-by-side and approach the throne of God. We pray for our days, our finances, our ministry, and each other's personal battles. We also pray for friends and family. For many years we saved the Christmas cards we had received. Each night after dinner, we selected two and prayed for those friends.

Scripture tells us that, where two or more gather in the name of Jesus, he is there (Matthew 18:20). When one of us travels for business or we spend a day apart, we often pray together by text, email, or phone. Sharing with God and each other what is uppermost on our hearts and minds deepens our understanding. Even when we stumble over words, placing our praises and petitions before our Lord increases our experience of oneness.

Oneness also includes physical and emotional intimacy. Chapter four will go into this in more detail. Spending quality time and sharing both daily life and special occasions together can also increase the sense of oneness. Often couples want this but struggle with the how-to. Chapter eleven has many suggestions for dates and celebrations.

When I drop something or my poor coordination takes center stage, we joke that CP must be contagious. Of course, it is not. Yet I have to embrace Jerry's disability in order to be one with him. Fighting against it, ignoring it, or overcompensating for his disability detracts from our unity. Suzanne Mintz, founder of the National Family Caregiver's Association, describes her life with Steven, diagnosed with multiple sclerosis (MS), like this: "He has clinical MS, but we both have MS."[2]

Whether you or your spouse had a disability when you married or acquired one afterward, oneness remains God's standard.[3] There is no biblical exemption for couples living with disability. As with other parts of a marriage including disability, oneness may look different in your marriage than in mine—it probably will. And that's okay. Thankfully, we're not the first ones to walk this road. But we have the perfect role model for our journey. Peter Rosenberger dedicated his book *Hope for the Caregiver*[4] to "Jesus Christ, Ultimate Caregiver to the Wounded Bride."

In this description of Jesus caring for us, we see one blessing in a marriage that involves disability. We have the beautiful privilege of being a living example of the love Jesus Christ has for his Church. Through our relationship, others will see how Jesus cares for, loves, and serves his body. They will observe how an imperfect body responds to love.

The apostle Paul tells us in Philippians 2:3–4 how to follow Christ's example. We are called to look not only to our own needs but also to the needs of our partner. Consider how our actions and thoughts may affect them. Act and speak to build up the person and the relationship.

The world of disability is open ended. Every person is one step, one breath, one heartbeat away from joining our ranks. Our growth in oneness shows the world that it's possible to not only survive but to thrive in a marriage that includes a disability.

While Isaac and Jill parented children with medical needs, their hands were full. They never expected that, a few years later, disability would also enter their marriage, but it did when Isaac received a diagnosis of multiple sclerosis. Now, over twenty years later, they share some things they learned about becoming one:

Jill: "Everyone should know we are on each other's team. There is no doubt we support each other, and people know we are there for one another. Allow the gift of loyalty to show through. See the value in each other. Live in an understanding way, even if you don't understand it. I don't have to get whatever is happening with Isaac, but I have to be understanding and kind because that's what Jesus would do."

Isaac: "We live a new normal, not like others. Not worse, just different. Sometimes in the crazy marriage cycle of ups and downs, it's hard to think the best about your spouse. As a man, I may hear my wife's helpful comments as criticism. I need to remember that she has my best in mind. Don't let the *D* word (divorce) enter your conversations. My diagnosis reminded me of our vows to love each other in sickness and in health. There were times I thought she'd be better without me, but marriage is a together commitment."

EMBRACING ONENESS

1. Set aside time to assess your oneness. How have you grown in this over the years? What still needs to develop? Face each other, and, using your own names, say together, "We are _____ and _____, another one of God's great ideas."
2. Have you and your spouse talked about the purpose of, or a vision for, your marriage? If not, set a time to explore this.
3. Do you pray together? What one step could you take to deepen your prayer life with one another?

EMBRACING YOUR FRIENDS

1. Don't lower expectations about marriage for your friends with disabilities. Encourage them to live and love according to the Bible's model.
2. Marriage is hard, and disability is relentless. Encourage your friends by positively mentioning the ways you see them becoming one.
3. Pray for your friends' marriages. You don't need to tell them. Just pray.

GENESIS 2:23-24

"The man said, 'This is now bone of my bones and flesh of my flesh; she shall be called "woman," for she was taken out of man.' That is why a man leaves his father and mother and is united to his wife, and they become one flesh."

PRAYER

Thank you, God, for my spouse. Thank you for the unique way you knit us together as individuals and brought us together in you. Show us how to deepen our life and love with each other and show you to the world around us. Amen.

TWO

SUBMIT OR DIE

After reading Ephesians 5, I whined to Jerry from my myopic point of view, "It's just not fair. The Bible says I need to submit twice—once to you and once to God."

My wise husband snickered. "Did you keep reading? You're told to submit twice, while all I have to do is *(read as a dire last-ditch effort to produce sound) . . . die!*"

His dramatic statement made the point. If he's willing to lay down his life for me, then submitting to him is comparatively easy. *Comparatively.*

To read this portion of God's Word properly, we must look at the context of the verses before the Ephesians 5 marital teaching.

Ephesians 4:17—5:20 begins with Paul reminding the reader that there is a need for change, a need to live a life transformed by God. When one embraces the life-altering teaching of Jesus, they agree to a new way to live. Paul tells us that these changes come with two actions: sloughing something off and replacing it with something new.

EPHESIANS 4:22—5:20	
Take Off / Be Done With	*Put On / Replace With*
Old way of living that is corrupt and deceitful (4:22)	New self, patterned after God's righteousness and holiness (4:23–24)
Falsehood and lies (4:25)	Speaking truthfully (4:25)
Anger to the point of sin (4:26)	Resolving anger before the sun goes down (4:26)
Giving the devil a foothold (4:27)	
Stealing (4:28)	Useful hands; sharing with those in need (4:28)
Unwholesome talk (4:29)	Words that help and build up others, that are beneficial to the listener (4:29)
Grieving the Holy Spirit (4:30)	
Bitterness, rage, anger, brawling, slander, malice (4:31)	Kindness, compassion, forgiveness (4:32)
	Walking in love following Christ's example (5:2)
Sexual immorality, impurity, greed (5:3)	
Obscenity, foolish talk, coarse joking (5:4)	Thanksgiving (5:4)
Living unwisely (5:15)	Living wisely; making the most of every opportunity (5:15, 16)
Foolishness (5:17)	Understanding God's will (5:17)
Getting drunk (5:18)	Being filled with the Spirit, as evidenced by psalms, hymns, and singing from our heart to the Lord while giving thanks (5:18–20)

These verses instruct *all* of Christ's followers how to live in *every* relationship.

I don't know about you, but I have miles to go before I'm proficient in letting go of my deceitful desires or always being kind, compassionate, and forgiving. Understanding God's will and consistently giving thanks are still works in progress in my life. I suspect that, if I regularly pursue these guidelines, I'll struggle less with the verses about submission in marriage.

The ten-verse section on biblical marriage and family life begins in Ephesians 5:21. The first nine words put our relationships in perspective: *submit to one another out of reverence for Christ*. The later admonition for a wife to live in submission to her husband follows instructions for every person in the body of Christ to submit to every other as an expression of our relationship with Jesus. This includes mutual submission to the authority of Christ between husband and wife. We submit when we yield to Christ's control and live in deference to one another.[5]

In *The Course of Love* Alain de Botton writes, "Being another's servant is not humiliating, quite the opposite, for it sets us free from the wearying responsibility of continuously catering to our own twisted, insatiable natures. We learn the relief and privilege of being granted something more important to live for than ourselves."

We warp Scripture and relationships when we relegate submission to being only about a wife's response to her husband. Whether or not we like it, God inspired these words. When we engage in biblical submission, first to Christ and next to those around us, we show Christ, his people, and the world that we love him and aren't focused on ourselves.

INSTRUCTIONS FOR MARRIAGE

"Submit to one another out of reverence for Christ.

"Wives, submit yourselves to your own husbands as you do to the Lord. For the husband is the head of the wife as Christ is the head of the church, his body, of which he is the Savior. Now as the church submits to Christ, so also wives should submit to their husbands in everything.

"Husbands, love your wives, just as Christ loved the church and gave himself up for her to make her holy, cleansing her by the washing with water through the word, and to present her to himself as a radiant church, without stain or wrinkle or any other blemish, but holy and blameless. In this same way, husbands ought to love their wives as their own bodies. He who loves his wife loves himself. After all, no one ever hated their own body, but they feed and care for their body, just as Christ does the church—for we are members of his body. "For this reason a man will leave his father and mother and be united to his wife, and the two will become one flesh." This is a profound mystery—but I am talking about Christ and the church. However, each one of you also must love his wife as he loves himself, and the wife must respect her husband."

—Ephesians 5:7–32

After we had read these verses together and were trying to grasp the truths, Jerry said to me, "I believe husbands *are* called to die. Perhaps not physically, but more likely to our own agendas, desires, careers, and even our calendars. We need to live our relationship with God as the top priority and our relationship with our wife is a very close second. This means that her growth and well-being are more important than my agenda, my career, my desires.

"I'm not trying to be a martyr, but in our self-absorbed world we are called to be others-absorbed. This is how husbands love wives . . . how I love you, Joan.

"I'd like to say that, because of my disability, I get a pass from dying to myself, but that's nowhere in Scripture. I'd like to be super successful in my career, run a flourishing business on the side, write, speak, teach . . . Not only would that be vanity, but it wouldn't prioritize *you*. I've had to die to some of my ambitions to make time to love and minister to you. It's not always easy. It's a death I'm called to choose daily."

Jerry calls submission being others-absorbed—thinking of and giving priority to the other. What wife wouldn't want to live in mutual submission to a man who believes and tries to practice that?

When our relationship was new and sprouting seeds of growth, I couldn't help but be Jerry-absorbed. In fact, my closest friends and coworkers probably grew tired of my heavy focus on this man. Thinking of submission as meaning that I would continue to think more of Jerry than I do of myself is a practical way for me to grasp this sometimes difficult concept.

How does submission shape our lives? We started before we were married. We had been friends and ministry associates for six years. The first time Jerry called me at home, instead of at the office, I sensed that something was changing, even though he spoke no words of affection. After we hung up, I told God I was going to take my hands off the relationship. I had dominated relationships in the past. If this one were to grow to more than friendship, it would have to be directed by God and Jerry. I didn't initiate calls to Jerry until several months later, when he invited me to. It seems to have worked; we recently celebrated our twenty-seventh anniversary.

In our day-to-day life, we often express mutual submission in little ways. We may see it in our expectations of each another. When Jerry must rise extra early for a long day of meetings, I don't whine about how early I'll have to get up to help him. When he gets home, I don't hammer him with my list of the day. I recognize his need for space as greater than my need to share.

Or it may be that he wants to watch a baseball game while the grocery store is calling my name. Noticing my weariness, he'll offer to shop with me and record the game or watch the end when we get home.

Jerry and I both have a good sense of humor. Often after one or both of us speak, someone else comments, "You must laugh all the time at home."

"You'd like to think so," we reply.

Humor can be a subtle reflection of how we love, honor, and respect one another. We each had one-liners or stories in our public speaking resources that could cast the broad class of men or women in a negative light. Some were jokes that were not a part of our experience but got a laugh if we attributed them to our spouse. The problem was that the listener didn't know if the anecdote was true. Sharing funny lines at the expense of each other might prevent others from understanding the admiration we share. Jerry and I agreed not to repeat a story, if true, without getting the other's permission in advance. We also agreed that we did not want to perpetuate stereotypes and would speak of marriage only positively.

Submission in our case doesn't mean that Jerry directs my every move or approves my expenditures. It's thinking first of the other—from my side, considering him before me. It's communicating honestly and frequently. It's recognizing the strength in the other and capitalizing on that, regardless of roles, particularly for those of us who live with disability in our marriage. The big idea of submission is lived out in little decisions all day long.

In our home I'm the practical or logistical leader. I'm the first one up and the last one to bed. If there's a sound during the night, I'm the one to check it out. Give me a challenge or an emergency, and I'll quickly assess the need and put a plan into action. However, if we're not mindful, this can become our de facto relational operating system, with me directing our lives.

But this isn't how I want to live. I don't believe that God gave Jerry to me so I could organize and plan his life. Certainly, there are areas in which I can be of help to him, and vice versa. I often say, "Jerry wears the pants in our family just as soon as I put them on him."

I can get hung up on the here and now and miss looking ahead, while Jerry, who is a visionary, sees the end goal. He understands what we need to relinquish in order to gain what we genuinely want. He identifies the mountain in the distance we need to conquer. Then I plot the path through the forest, around the rocks, and across the river standing between us and the mountain. This is how our teamwork functions.

Jerry took a long route to earn his master's degree. After multiple starts and stops in his single life and a couple of random classes soon after we married, he was ready to get his coursework finished. He selected a program at a university about an hour away. His classes meant full weekends and some weeknights.

We discussed how to make our lives and schedules fit his program. We intentionally cut out all extra activities at work and church and stopped travel. He gave up watching baseball and college basketball (this was how I knew he was serious). I agreed to type his papers as he dictated them to me. These changes were life altering but also temporary. This was the route we navigated to get him to the mountain out yonder. And it worked. What a joyous day it was when he crossed the stage to accept his diploma.

Over the years, two memories stand out of times when we didn't see eye-to-eye on how to handle decisions. Both involved planning cross-country moves. Each time we spent hours talking, trying to convince each other that our way was the best. And in both situations I experienced a clear message from God to move out of the way and trust my husband. As I obeyed God's prompting, the process became clearer, and our resolve to work together in the same direction grew stronger.

I remember driving to ladies' Bible study one night, pondering Jerry's words to me over dinner. He was between jobs, and we were living on a tight budget. A move from California to Pennsylvania appeared to be imminent. He said that God had told him, "I've got you—watch."

That was it: God has got us, so watch. While driving, I was telling God that I could agree with the part that he would take care of us. But watch? No way. There was too much that had to be done. Watching might work for Jerry but not for me. I literally felt a gentle slap across my face and heard, "Why is it you can trust my voice through your husband when you perceive it is good. But it's not okay when the message means that you have to change what you're doing and watch?"

Ouch. I drove to my girlfriend's house where we were meeting and told her the story, and we prayed together for me to submit to God's leading of our family.

"Submission is definitely a dance," Jill reflected. "For example, we value praying together. We'd like to every night, but my husband never remembers. and I get angry that he forgets something so spiritually important. I know it's not because he doesn't care or find worth in prayer. Memory loss from his disability means that he needs support to make it happen. I had to wrestle with God about my role of support in this. I don't have it down yet."

For Isaac, leading and mutual submission meant trying not to fall apart. "My behaviors didn't make home a safe place for my family because my cognitive issues work like dementia. When a thought leaves my head, it's gone. I'd come home from church with one kid instead of two. Once I went to pick our daughter up from a pool party. I talked with the parents while she went to get a towel. And then I left—without her. The parents called me to see what had happened. When you don't understand yourself, it's difficult to help someone else. I'm selfish, even though I try not to be. That submission part of role change and trying to understand what God was doing blindsided me. For a long time, I wanted to understand. I wanted Jill to fix everything, but I still wanted her to be my wife."

Jill concludes, "In the middle of this changing dance, it's easy to get lost, tired, and frustrated."

EMBRACING SUBMISSION

1. Husbands, how are you doing at dying? Does your wife know that, after Christ Jesus, she is the most important person in the world to you? It will take more than words to convince her.
2. Wives, respecting our husbands is a large part of submission. We broadcast our tones and attitudes even when we think we don't. How can you respect your husband with your spoken and unspoken communication?
3. How does disability impact your thoughts and actions around submission?

EMBRACING YOUR FRIENDS

1. Sometimes disability divides a family. Encourage your friends who live with disability to live their life journey together.
2. We can forget sometimes that life isn't always harder because of disability; sometimes life is hard just because we are human in a fallen world. Help us remember that some of these struggles, like submission, dying to self, and respect are hard for most everyone.

1 PETER 5:6

"Humble yourselves, therefore, under God's mighty hand, that he may lift you up in due time."

PRAYER

Father, submission is a word that carries a great deal of baggage in our culture. Would you please teach us anew what it means to submit to you and to one another in love? Empower us by your Spirit to follow your example. Amen.

THREE

VOWS AND DREAMS

Shelley and I chatted about the difference in our marriages. I married a man with a known disability, and she didn't. Yet her groom incurred an illness that has severely limited his body and mind. This has changed their lifestyle. She had never considered that a disability could become part of their lives and now lives with shattered dreams.

Our wedding guests commented on their realization that, at some point, they might be in our situation. Actually, their comments were more along the lines of how they *had never* considered being in a similar situation. Witnessing Jerry and me sitting on stage, facing one another and promising to love and serve each other, knowing disability to be part of our lives, made them think. Many told us that, while they had never considered that a long-term illness or disability might one day rock their world, they had watched us commit to a "happy ever after" that would look much different from theirs.

Most couples promise to love one another "for better or worse, for richer or poorer, in sickness and in health." But the majority think of challenges in terms of a job change, a fight, the flu, or morning sickness. Beginning marriage with a visible, lifelong physical need does not seem to many to qualify as "better," "richer," or "in health." Our reality gave them pause to think.

Isaac and Jill Penney married on a sunny fall day. The minister stated that God would use their love in a unique way. While they thought "that was cool to hear," their premarital discussions had never pointed in that direction. They had no inkling of the multiple ways in which disability would enter their lives in the years ahead. Later, the officiant commented that this message had kept coming to him. Isaac and Jill didn't at the time understand the ramifications of the special love or the prophetic statement. Isaac felt as though the minister's words detracted from the typical ceremony, and this made him angry.

While Shelley and her husband, and the Penneys, encountered life-changing circumstances that altered their hopes and dreams, Jerry and I did, too. Our situation and expectations were different, but our outcome has been similar.

How should we handle the death of dreams within our marriage? I suggest two practices. The first is to look back at the vows you made to one another in your wedding. The second is to reflect on the hopes that brought you together. Thank God for those that were fulfilled, and dream again for your new reality.

VOWS

Vows aren't just words we speak to move the ceremony along to get to the reception. They are the foundation upon which we commit to building our relationship. Whether you have a large public ceremony or a few minutes with a justice of the peace, brides and grooms speak promises in the presence of God and witnesses. How we live out those pledges forms the foundation of our marriage and speaks to those around us.

Perhaps you used the traditional vows in your ceremony: "I, _____, take thee, _____, to be my wedded wife/husband, to have and to hold from this day forward, for better, for worse, for richer, for poorer, in sickness and in health, to love and to cherish till death do us part, according to God's holy ordinance; and thereto I pledge thee my faith."

Don't let the old English trick you into thinking these words don't pack a punch. Lives may change in terms of health, jobs, ministries, hobbies, communities, and friendships, but the constant is the couple. When days or months are hard, vows commit in advance for you to face difficulties and challenges together.

Jerry and I wrote our own vows:

"Joan, I love you. I thank God for you and our love. I will follow Christ's example in the leadership of our home. I promise before our Lord to honor and cherish you above all other human relationships. I will encourage you, comfort you, protect and provide for you as God gives me grace and strength. I will pray with you and for you. I choose today to commit my life and love to you until God calls us home."

"Jerry, I love you. I thank God for you and our love. I promise before our Lord to encourage you, comfort you, serve you, and support you in all that you do. I will respect you, honor you, and submit to your leadership under Christ. I promise to give you understanding and patience and to pray with you and for you. I choose today to commit my life and love to you until God calls us home."

Like the traditional vows, our pledges reflect our understanding of God's plan for marriage and our desire to put aside our egos. Nearly three decades later, we are still a work in progress, but recalling what we promised refreshes our distracted minds and marriage.

One way we kept our vows fresh in our memories was to read them together every month for our first few years. Now we're more likely to read them on our anniversary.

When life challenges arise unexpectedly, review your promises. When I do, I find that these disturbances often point out a laxity in my prayer life or the intrusion of petty annoyances I've allowed to eat away at my respect and honor for Jerry. Often, the remedy is to spend more time together.

RENEWING FORGOTTEN VOWS

There may be a day when one of us can no longer articulate our vows. I hope that, if that time comes, we will remember this story from social media, credited to Anne Duncan:

> Something wonderful happened recently. My wonderful husband of 12 years, Bill, told me he wanted to marry me. Now, as most of you reading this will know, Bill has been living with dementia for 9 years. For the past year, Bill has been unaware of our relationship and no longer knows my name.

When Bill told me he, "Really REALLY liked me and wanted to be with me forever"—I was really touched. Bill doesn't use many words now and finds it hard to express himself, but I got lots of kisses and hugs as I accepted his "proposal." It was so lovely. Another memory to treasure.

What I wasn't prepared for was that he'd remember it the next day. He wanted to know when we were getting married. This was Thursday, and as I was having my "close girlfriends" round on the Saturday, I suggested that was a good day.

My daughter Andrea said I needed a dress. Really? "Of course," she said. "How else can it be a wedding?"

I got a dress that afternoon, expecting to return it unworn. But Bill still remembered on Friday. Together we bought a special cake. My cousin Lynne gave me flowers for my hair. Eva prepared our renewal of vows with a special bit for Bill, so he felt we were getting married.

The next day, with homemade bunting, a beautiful flower arrangement and bouquet, stunning weather, and our wonderful family, Bill and I got married again.

It was the most wonderful day. We are so blessed to be supported by family and close friends who love us both and do everything they can to help Bill and me enjoy our lives together. I never dreamed we would renew our vows, but we did. And it was wonderful. Bill was wonderful. And what is even more amazing is that two weeks later, Bill still thinks he just married his new girlfriend, and it makes him very happy.

You can never assume that, just because someone has advanced dementia with all the difficulties that presents, they can't still surprise you in the most unlikely ways. Bill has made me very happy yet again.

DREAMS THAT DREW YOU TOGETHER

Why did you marry your spouse? Many believe they've found just the right man or woman. When Jerry told a friend he met all the criteria I asked God for in a husband, his friend commented, "I guess she didn't have an extensive list. Maybe just a man who is breathing?"

Contrary to his friend's tongue-in-cheek remark, I married the man of my dreams, and he is much more than just breathing. Jerry is an overcomer with a quick and witty sense of humor. He's full of passion, integrity, and a deepening love for God and me. Simply put, he's the man God created to be my Junior Shepherd here on earth.

This explains why I chose Jerry. But why did he choose me? He might say because when I visited (we lived three time zones apart), I stocked his freezer with homemade dinners to entice him to avoid fast food and encourage better nutrition. His married friends told him that alone was reason to marry me. Hopefully, that wasn't the *only* factor.

Using a power wheelchair is only one facet of Jerry's life. Admittedly, it is significant. We don't downplay the effect of disability because it has a profound impact on every area of our relationship. But he, like your spouse, is much more than his disability. Perhaps in learning to overcome challenges, God prepared him to marry a strong-willed, independent woman. I'm grateful that my often-rough-edged character flaws didn't scare him away.

Jerry is an ambitious soul. He has never pulled back from hard times or missed an opportunity to speak up about injustice. His mom claimed that he was born with a suitcase in his hand—ready to move out and take on the world. He evidenced this the day he entered the first grade.

After only one morning in the classroom, his mom picked him up and took him home. Expecting to enjoy lunch and go back to school, he was surprised when she sat him in front of the television. He asked her why. She explained, "We thought it would be good for you to try a half day and, if that went well, work up to a full day."

He quickly realized that, by attending only half days, he would be gray before he graduated. Plus, he had successfully completed half-day kindergarten the year before. Little Jerry responded, "Wouldn't it be better to try a full day and, if that doesn't work, cut back to a half day?" His mom took him back to school and told the teacher, "He's all yours."

Psalm 139 speaks of the purposeful design in each person's creation. For some, that means encountering disability from birth. For others, disability unfolds much later when an accident or illness occurs. Yet others may never find their lives directly touched by disability. This psalm, in concert with Genesis 1:27, assures us that each person bears the image of God. Since disability is how God purposefully knits some people together, we know that his image isn't reflected in our bodies, our intellectual capabilities, or our language skills. Instead, it is the very breath of God in our souls, our innermost beings, that makes us who we are.

Our marriage looks nothing like what we see portrayed in Hollywood, but then, whose does? Disability means that our family looks different from that of many of our able-bodied friends. Yet God's design and purpose for our life together does not differ from that of anyone else; the difference is in how we work out that design.

When the day-to-day realities of life wear me down, or I'm tired of the impact of disability, I reflect on what drew me to love this man. On those days when our communication keeps missing, or I'm frustrated with his drive, I recall who I know him to be: an image-bearer who doesn't intentionally irritate me. That isn't his character.

When we know we are moving into a busy or stressful phase of life, one of us is likely to comment, "Let's remember we're on the same team. Even though things may feel out of control for a time, let's assume the best of each other in our conversations and comments."

If disability has changed your spouse, many of the things you first loved probably remain intact, despite the overshadowing of a medical condition. Look for manifestations of their personality and glimmers of their character that drew you to them.

DREAMING INTO THE FUTURE

Jerry and I spent hours on our dates and through our engagement talking about how we would minister, serve, and travel together. We considered how his life would become easier and he'd gain time in his day because I'd help with his personal care. I'd assist him in doing physical therapy exercises to extend his functional abilities. We planned that I would continue to camp with friends and travel on international mission trips with his blessing. The pictures we created in our heads were beautiful, fully accessible, and free of bumps in the road.

Working and ministering together? We've done that for half of our married life. While this was exciting, memorable, and fulfilling, we've learned how competitive we each are. Our reality looks little like the picture we'd imagined.

Assisting with personal care and therapy routines? We didn't expect that, several years into our marriage, I'd need therapy exercises to maintain my ability to help him. If we both did all the stretching recommended for our various body parts, this activity would fill every day. So, we pick and choose. Helping him with his routine diminished my previously free and flexible schedule and added wear and tear to my body.

Traveling? In our first twenty years we traveled around the country and enjoyed brief ventures to some islands accessible by cruise ship. International mission trips for me haven't continued as we'd hoped. God impressed on me that this is not my time to go overseas, even if it is for kingdom work. I pushed back and fought against that—with God, not Jerry—but God held firm. My place, my job, my primary ministry is to and with my husband.

Our marriage looks very little like what we'd expected during our engagement, but this doesn't mean it isn't beautiful. My picture of beauty has changed. Realistically acknowledging and dealing with bumps—even enormous obstacles—contributes to my new view of true beauty. I value rugged strength, not a flawless exterior.

It has been healthy for me to acknowledge that I, too, have experienced the death of certain goals. But perhaps some were simply dreams. What God has granted us in place of those is a stronger appreciation of and love for one another, a deeper understanding of what is important in life, and gratitude for the time and opportunities we have. Oh, and he gave us new visions to consider.

The changing of our dreams and expectations is not unlike what the people of Judah experienced when Jerusalem fell and they found themselves in Babylon. Jeremiah 29:4–7 records instructions that God, through the prophet Jeremiah, gave to the captives:

> "This is what the LORD Almighty, the God of Israel, says to all those I carried into exile from Jerusalem to Babylon: 'Build houses and settle down; plant gardens and eat what they produce. Marry and have sons and daughters; find wives for your sons and give your daughters in marriage, so that they too may have sons and daughters. Increase in number there; do not decrease. Also, seek the peace and prosperity of the city to which I have carried you into exile. Pray to the LORD for it, because if it prospers, you too will prosper.'"

Your marriage may differ from the way you had envisioned it. Caring for a spouse with a disability is not what you had signed up for. Fighting this reality will exhaust you and hinder your moving forward. Follow Jeremiah's words and settle in for the long haul. Accept and embrace your new life. The bounty and blessing may just surprise you.

Looking forward to new goals resembles watching a child grow. We have a great niece who, in her primary years, aspired to be a fairy scientist. And, the next year, an astronaut dancer. Perhaps by the time she has to decide, those will be viable career paths. More likely, though, over the next ten years her desires will morph and change to ones more aligned with her maturing personality, strengths, and interests.

There's nothing wrong with discussing wild fairy scientist or astronaut dancer dreams with your spouse. But, with maturity and deeper knowledge of each other, learn to relinquish the aspirations that may block your joy by adapting to your current health and financial realities.

I no longer go tent camping, and Jerry's idea of roughing it is the Holiday Inn Express, but we still serve at camps together each summer. Our desire for a counseling practice has become a ministry of mentoring and coaching people with disabilities and encouraging caregivers. Our travels focus on seeing the many people we love more than on exploring new vistas.

SOME DREAMS DON'T CHANGE

Jerry is no fair-weather baseball fan. He has stayed true to the Detroit Tigers through their many years of downs and a few ups. After moving back to the east coast, we have been able to make occasional trips to see his beloved team during spring training in central Florida. On one trip, after surveying the stadium and surrounding fields, he picked out a tree under which he thought he could see the team on all three practice fields. He told me, "Someday that tree will bear a plaque saying 'Reserved for Jerry Borton.'"

The brass sign is not on the tree (yet), but if you get to the stadium in February or March, look for him along the first-base line. Perhaps some of those wishes still live on.

EMBRACING YOUR VOWS AND DREAMS

1. Dust off your wedding vows or watch the video of your ceremony. Then sit face-to-face with your spouse and commit afresh to the promises you first made. Talk about how you (not your spouse) are doing in terms of keeping them.
2. If you realize that your wedding vows weren't as substantive as you'd like, or you can't find or remember them, rewrite them. Then sit face-to-face with your partner and tell them what you commit to from that day forward.
3. How has God taken what may have been the death of one or more of your dreams and traded it for a new kind of beauty? What new aspirations do you share for your future?

EMBRACING YOUR FRIENDS

1. Encourage your couple friends who live with disability to dream together in their journey. Resist the urge to comment on how realistic these dreams may be.
2. Tell your friends how their marriage and relationship encourage you in your own marriage.
3. If your friend is struggling with the impact of a new disability on their marriage, ask about what attracted them to their spouse in the early years and help them see that their loved one is still there.

PROVERBS 19:21

"Many are the plans in a person's heart, but it is the Lord's purpose that prevails."

PRAYER

Father God, you teach us to not take vows lightly. Please forgive us for the areas where we've neglected our promises to one another. Renew our commitment to live together for you. Thank you for the gift of imagination and for the visions that haven't come to reality. Show us the new ones you have for us. Amen.

FOUR

INTIMACY

What does *intimacy* mean to you? Many consider the word a euphemism or synonym for the act of sex, but sex alone isn't intimacy. In fact, people who work in the sex industry admit to the lack of intimacy in their experience.[6]

Definitions of *intimacy* include "A close, familiar, and usually affectionate or loving personal relationship with another person or group." In addition, the word means "a close association with or detailed knowledge or deep understanding of a place, subject, period of history, etc."[7]

When I use the word *intimacy*, I am referring to a loving relationship built on a deep understanding of one another.

While many enter marriage focused on physical engagement, sex is not the only way a couple can achieve closeness. A quick internet search reveals that many counselors, sociologists, and professors write about this topic.

I propose that the richest sexual intimacy results from developing closeness and authenticity with your husband or wife in the emotional, mental, physical, and spiritual realms. This correlates with the way Jesus told us to love God in Mark 12:30: "Love the Lord your God with all your heart and with all your soul and with all your mind and with all your strength."

EMOTIONAL INTIMACY

We can sum up emotional intimacy in three words: *vulnerable, honest communication.*

As your relationship grows from the first date, you'll want to share with your beloved more of your experiences and feelings. You might see or experience something and think, *I can't wait to tell ____ about it.* This shows a desire for emotional intimacy. If the name you inserted is that of someone other than your spouse, you need to evaluate where you're putting your attention. Even if your spouse can no longer verbally communicate, continue to share your life in small segments. This will remind you of your commitment. We know that people can continue to hear and process even when they struggle to speak. For some, it may be an incredible blessing of trust and acceptance when you still talk to them.

You may wonder if your words will confuse your spouse. You may feel that you can't share certain details any longer. If this describes your situation, use a journal or create a document on your computer and record your thoughts, just as though you were speaking to your beloved. You may also benefit from professional or pastoral counseling to help you process these changes. Another option is to consider a caregivers' support group.

A word of caution: beware of sharing deeply with someone else of the opposite sex while you are both still married to another. This can create a level of emotional intimacy that draws you away from your spouse.

Growing in your emotional relationship means that you and your spouse know all about each other. You can relate your embarrassing moments and those experiences you can't confide to anyone else. You trust them completely. Neither of you would reveal information that would embarrass or humiliate the other.

Emotional intimacy requires time to grow more deeply in trust and openness and to focus on one another. Sometimes, after a busy day of appointments, I get home and immediately start cooking dinner. Jerry may roll into the kitchen and ask about my day or a particular part of it. I don't want to withhold information, but I need some space to think through my day before I can talk through it with him. Cooking dinner gives me that time. A brusque reply of "good" may imply that I don't want to talk; better might be "I don't want to talk right now" or "Let's talk later." So, I say, "It was good, but can I get dinner in the oven and then sit and talk?" He understands that I need a bit of a break first.

Emotional intimacy allows couples to exchange only a glance in public and know what the other is thinking. We can also feel safe in this space sharing our worries and our joys. Evaluate your maturity by how readily you two resolve disagreements. Are you quick to forgive? Are you willing to apologize?

Sometimes Jerry and I misunderstand each other. Our words and the manner in which they're spoken create a mixed impression, leading to frustration, isolation, and an indifferent attitude.

When this happens, one of us will often remind the other, "We're on the same team. We don't intend to irritate. Let's take a breath and try again." This is also a time when we each apologize for harsh tones and unfair words.

There's no substitute for time spent building emotional intimacy.[8] Doing so creates not only a more pleasant daily life but also a foundation of honest trust that will sustain the relationship when a crisis arises.

SPIRITUAL INTIMACY

Spiritual intimacy may be one of the most difficult areas to establish, but I believe it carries the greatest blessing.[9] Sharing the same faith allows a couple to approach life with united values. This creates a foundation for decision making. It doesn't make decisions easy but offers common ground and similar standards with which to evaluate choices.

Praying with your spouse, as mentioned earlier, is so essential to spiritual intimacy that it bears revisiting. Praying with Jerry has long been one of my most cherished times with him. We say things in prayer that we may not already have discussed. Perhaps we didn't think about, or think through, an issue, or perhaps talking to God together opens a new level of vulnerability.

This practice reminds each of us of what concerns dominate our thoughts and desires. Jerry hears my stumbling words when I try to articulate hard things. He hears my struggle when I tell God what I know I should—but don't necessarily want to or feel as though I can—do. He empathizes when God touches me, and I pray through tears. And I've learned to respond in the same way to him.

Sometimes, after praying, one of us will ask the other whether we want to talk more about a certain subject. Sometimes we do, but not always. Either way is okay.

Work against the temptation to lay out your agenda for your spouse under the guise of prayer. That's manipulation, not spiritual intimacy.

Reading the Bible together is another way to grow closer. Discussing what we read offers us the opportunity to discern the meaning of the text and explore how we can apply it to our lives.

In our early years we read the devotional *Quiet Times for Couples* by Norman Wright each night after dinner. As we learned to live together, the points we pondered after each reading offered invaluable wisdom.

Worshiping together in corporate situations, small groups, or individual settings offers another building block of spiritual intimacy. When we were first married, I asked Jerry if he preferred for me to sit with him or stand with the congregation when singing. Initially, he said it would be nice if I sat with him, although he later offered that I could do as I wished. I enjoy feeling that we are on a level field as we turn our hearts to worship when I sit beside him.

Worship need not and should not be confined to Sundays. One of us may stream one or more of our favorite Christian artists as we pursue our activities of the day. This focuses our minds on Jesus.

It's not just music that inspires worship. I may point out a stunning sunset or a majestic mountain view as we drive. Jerry may mention how a person was unusually kind in an interaction. Those are opportunities to thank and praise God, training our focus back on him.

Service projects and short-term mission trips can constitute a spiritual intimacy boot camp. We may serve food at a local mission, play games with inner-city kids, or teach Bible studies during a week of camp. Each such opportunity, however, usually requires more of us than we feel we have to give. Yet we find the energy to serve when we take our eyes off our own lives and work toward a common goal in the name of Jesus. Serving together offers accountability and provides points for prayer in our devotional time.

Grace and Philip were engaged when he took a dive into a shallow pool and broke his neck. After he had completed rehab therapy, they fulfilled their desire and commitment to marry. Each had been active in serving God before they met, and that priority continued. Immediately, they began serving in the church nursery together.

Grace shared, "Later, when we joined a church as a married couple, we began teaching Sunday school together. And we still do that. We help each other with the disability ministries at our church. I am often the hands, and Philip is the tech guy behind the scenes. Serving is a good way to get your mind off self, and serving God together is a good way to get your mind off your problems that disability brings to a marriage."

INTELLECTUAL INTIMACY

Intellectual intimacy involves learning together and spurring one another on to growth. I'm glad that Jerry and I are both avid readers. He reads any book he can find and every one recommended, especially about leadership, personal development, coaching, and baseball. In fact, his town's librarian tells of having frequently searched other library databases to secure new baseball books after he had, as a boy, read all the ones she had.

I prefer to read fiction. Since we met, Jerry has probably read two fiction books, because I heartily recommended them or asked him to. When traveling we often listen to non-fiction books. This gives us the opportunity to discuss them, helping me see the main points. We learn from different authors and share user-friendly portions with each other. Sometimes—particularly for road trips—we select a book about marriage or another topic of mutual interest.

Other activities that develop intellectual intimacy involve learning new things together. It may be a hobby, craft, or language. Perhaps you take a cooking class together or watch a movie or docudrama that piques your mutual interest. These activities provide conversation starters and often become the fodder for fun memories.

Have you ever considered expanding your cultural horizons together? Jerry and I don't view ourselves as people of high culture. For instance, you'll rarely hear classical music in our home, unless a niece or my sister performs. The pictures in our home aren't by artists anyone outside our circles would recognize. Rather, they are paintings and quilts created by friends and family that together tell a story of our lives. The walls of the little corner in which I write are laden with artifacts from international trips I or loved ones have taken.

We've dined only once at a restaurant where the server placed the napkins on our laps (and that was when someone else paid). We're more likely to ask for extra napkins when we pick up our ribs at the local barbecue hole-in-the-wall. But every year we explore a couple of venues outside our normal comfort zone. We may visit an art museum, attend a symphony concert, or take a cooking class. Often, we find new things to enjoy. When was the last time you and your spouse learned something new together?

PHYSICAL INTIMACY

Physical intimacy may arguably be the most fun to work on, but it still takes time, particularly when disability is in the picture. It is so much more than the act of intercourse. Hand holding, massages, hugs, and kisses are not just foreplay. Even some of the personal acts of a spouse caring for the other's physical needs involve a deep level of intimacy. Yet other caregivers can conduct that same act or service without invoking physical intimacy.

Start by being comfortable in your own skin, whether or not disability is part of your experience. Are you thankful for the body God gave you? Are you grateful to have a spouse who accepts and loves your body? If you're dissatisfied with your physical body, can you work together to change it? Try walking or exercising together. Share a revised dietary plan. Explore new things. Sharing your victories and the hard spots of your physical life can work to meld your spirits, too.

When one of you can't leave the house, or a care facility,[10] hold hands often. Look into your loved one's eyes when you tell them of your love. Remind them that they have the bluest eyes or most beautiful hair you've ever seen. Appreciate the strength they still have and use, even if only to roll over in bed. Take lotion when you visit to rub on their hands or feet.

One way to keep your marriage strong is to stop what you are doing when your spouse returns home long enough to greet him or her with a kiss. How long and how often do you kiss? The "Ripley's Believe It or Not"[11] world record, set in 2013, is held by a couple in Thailand. Their one kiss lasted fifty-eight hours, thirty-five minutes, and fifty-eight seconds. I have to wonder why it couldn't have lasted two more seconds to make it to thirty-six minutes, but . . .

Few will seek that record. But we *can* beat the national average,[12] which claims that many couples go for up to a week without kissing. When they do, they're likely to share only a quick peck, lasting mere seconds.

Many years ago, I listened to a radio talk show guest suggesting that couples should kiss for at least ten seconds.[13] That seems brief—until you try it. The first few times I did so, I didn't tell Jerry what I was doing. I kept a silent count in my head, but he didn't seem to notice or mind. With practice, I found that I didn't need to track with an internal timer. I can't say we remember or practice this suggestion regularly, but when we do, it's worth it. Would you excuse me for a moment while I take a ten-second break right now?

The act of joining two bodies as one in intercourse, within the context of a committed marriage, provides the greatest physical intimacy. If you are hoping I'll share some techniques, I am sorry to disappoint you. The uniqueness of each person and disability, and the fact that I'm not trained in this area, prevent my doing so. Talk with your doctor or physical therapist and ask for resources. If you know of a rehab hospital (not a nursing home, but true rehab) or a university teaching hospital, ask there. The appendix lists some helpful resources.

One challenge to intimacy for those of us living with a disability in our marriage is time. We may feel as though there are not enough hours in the day to grow with our spouse intellectually, spiritually, or emotionally. We're too busy living and caregiving. We may try to rush physical intimacy to fulfill our own longings. Yet without emotional, spiritual, and intellectual closeness, physical acts yield intimacy only briefly, if at all.

Our intimacy is not the way it is depicted on TV or in the movies. I suspect that is true for others, too, not just those of us dealing with disability. We had to release the mental images of a smoothly coordinated act and learn to love one another in a way that works for us. This may involve rescheduling personal care needs if they distract the caregiving spouse from physical intimacy.

There are times we plan for the act of lovemaking, even days or weeks out. We know it ahead of time—this day and time. That may sound unromantic. For us, though, scheduling aids our romance as we anticipate and prioritize our time together.

EMBRACING INTIMACY
1. Make time to sit with your spouse and talk through the four areas of intimacy. Which areas are working well for you? Is there a goal you could make toward improvement?
2. Assess yourself to determine if you are transferring an area of unsatisfied intimacy with your beloved to a person outside your marriage, including a parent or child.
3. Discuss with your spouse the idea of scheduling romantic interludes.

EMBRACING YOUR FRIENDS
1. If you notice or sense that your friend is practicing unhealthy intimacy outside their marriage, talk with them about it.
2. Share resources you and your spouse have found helpful, even if you're unsure how they might apply to another couple.
3. Invite your friends on a double date to explore a new area, such as art, music, sports, or cooking.

MARK 10:6-9
"'At the beginning of creation God "made them male and female." For this reason a man will leave his father and mother and be united to his wife, and the two will become one flesh. So they are no longer two, but one flesh. Therefore what God has joined together, let no one separate.'"

PRAYER
Thank you, God, for creating us for relationship with you and with other people. Today I am grateful for the gift of intimacy with my spouse. Show me how I can love my partner more and grow with them emotionally, intellectually, spiritually, and physically. Amen.

SECTION TWO

THE DAILINESS OF DISABILITY

FIVE

ADJUSTMENTS

"What was your hardest adjustment in marriage?" we're frequently asked.

The questioner expects an answer related to personal care issues, accessibility, or relationship intimacy. We've experienced adjustments in each of those areas, but they weren't our biggest. Not even close. That honor goes to . . . (can you hear the drum roll?) . . . driving. I don't mean *how* to drive a wheelchair accessible van; I was skilled in driving a twenty-five-passenger bus before we were married.

Simply put, I *know* I'm the better driver. Funny thing, though: Jerry *thinks* he's better. A periodic fender bender or speeding ticket on each of our records with similar frequency rules out the law as a determining standard.

Jerry thinks I push the gas pedal beyond its natural capabilities and don't take turns smoothly enough. I believe he drives at a snail's pace . . . until he approaches a stop sign or slow-moving vehicle, at which point I am convinced he speeds up prior to screeching to a halt.

We both can drive our van. In our previous vehicle, when I drove he rode in the open section behind the driver's seat, giving him a bird's-eye view of the dashboard. On long trips he would periodically remind me, "If you get a ticket, it comes out of your money." Thankfully, our new van allows us to sit side by side.

When he drives, I sit in the passenger seat, giving me a perfect view of the road conditions. Somehow that position activates the driving coach in me. I frequently let him know when I think he's over a line, not driving safely, or exhibiting any other perceived traffic violation. Stomping on my invisible brake while exhibiting my fine command of sound effects—"Oooh, aaahh, slow down, and watch out"—prompts Jerry to caution me that my reactions might become the cause of an accident.

You might think this is funny. At times it is. Driving together has been the longest running and greatest challenge of our life together. We didn't have to face it until marriage because we had dated long distance. During our limited in-person dates, driving was the furthest thing from our minds. Before I tell you how we remedied this problem, grab a cup of tea or coffee and enjoy two stories, shared with Jerry's blessing, that confer some authority on my claims.

While single, Jerry went to a wedding several hours from his home. Because he got a late start, he knew he had to pick up the pace. He had driven the road many times before and had never seen police activity. Suddenly, he noticed red and blue flashing lights behind him. When he pulled over to allow them to pass, six patrol cars also pulled over and surrounded his van. The officer who came to his window asked if Jerry knew how long he'd been following him. "No, sir." He was shocked to hear the answer: "About nine miles." When Jerry did not pull over, the officer had called for backup. This was the day after the OJ Simpson chase seen around the world.

The officers faced a dilemma. The state law read that, if multiple patrol cars were needed to stop a vehicle, the driver had to be taken to the station and booked. These officers didn't have a wheelchair accessible paddy wagon, and Jerry's van didn't have a driver's seat, nor did the officers know how to drive with hand controls. The cadre of patrolmen conferred for a long time, enough to allow Jerry to build up a heavy dose of stress and miss the wedding. The first officer came back to him and asked, "Son, what is the speed limit?"

"Fifty-five, sir."

"Son, do you think you can drive that speed?"

"Yes, sir."

With that, the officer released him to continue on his way. Jerry slowly reentered the highway without even a written warning. Any paperwork would've reflected the number of officers involved who didn't follow protocol.

Perhaps you think you understand why he drives more slowly than I do. Read on.

Another time he got stopped for going too slowly. I was in the van because we had just gotten married and were driving to our honeymoon. *Have you ever heard of someone who drove too slowly on their honeymoon?*

To his credit, Jerry reminds me that mountains rose on the right, and the road had a steep drop-off to the ocean on the left. He wanted to make it to our honeymoon without an accident, and driving slowly seemed the right choice. The off-duty police officer behind us wanted to get home, and there was no place for him to pass. We began our life together with the memory of a traffic warning and of allowing the officer to leave before we got back on the road.

Why do I tell Jerry's stories here and not mine? He explains that one challenge a person with a disability faces is the perception on the part of others that they're a super saint—always smiling, happy, and never wrong. Others assume that disability is enough to bear, without the person doing inappropriate things or, even worse, sinning. Jerry and I will be the first to tell you that we both sin and fall short of God's expectations for us (Romans 3:23) as well as of our expectations for one another.

IT'S NOT ALL ABOUT DISABILITY

One quandary of family life with disability is discerning which experiences relate to disability and which are simply typical of life. I still marvel at Jerry's admission in our early years of failing to understand that some obstacles he faced were similar to those confronting other people, too. He had grown up assuming that everything he encountered related to his CP, but issues with driving, ego, and finances, as well as job concerns and family pressures, are common to all. Disability may increase the stress or alter the way we address these concerns, but it is often not the major source of our challenges.

Parents of kids with disabilities sometimes contact me to pose a scenario and ask a question, hoping I can share advice. Often, especially for first-time parents, I respond with something like "Congratulations. Your child is experiencing a typical and very normal part of childhood. It has nothing to do with a disability, and everything to do with being an adolescent."

Traces of disability seep into all areas of life and can magnify or muddy our perspective on everything else. Reality checks with family members or close friends are helpful in determining what might be a typical challenge unrelated to disability.

My wise friend Grace, who is a few years further ahead in marriage, reminded me, "No matter how long you are married, there will always be something new to catch you by surprise. Whether it is physical problems or a supply issue related to the disability, it keeps you on your toes. You simply cannot coast, thinking you have it all figured out. It also keeps you depending on God."

ACKNOWLEDGING FAMILY DIFFERENCES

We had both grown up in game-playing families (table games, that is). Several weeks after our honeymoon, we played a game while the chocolate, garlic, and peppers in Jerry's favorite meal, Cincinnati Chili, simmered on the stove.

Both of our families played canasta, and on this day, just a few hands in, I realized that I had missed a significant play. Unfortunately, Jerry noticed, too, and capitalized on my error. This "whooping" continued until I had no hope of winning.

Big crocodile tears streamed down my face.

"What's wrong? What happened? What did I do?" my rookie husband pleaded.

Once I had composed myself enough to talk, we learned that our families' playing cultures were unique. In the Borton family, if your opponent made a mistake, you took full advantage of it. The Morris family, on the other hand, played with the unwritten rule that, if someone made a mistake, you could make the most of it for a brief round or two, but eventually you'd let the person back in to join the fun.

This probably wasn't the first, and it surely wouldn't be the last, time we bumped up against family history and expectations. At least the chili did not disappoint.

FAMILIARITY BREEDS CARELESSNESS

After several years, couples may take their relationship for granted. We think we've figured each other out and plod along mindlessly. Renting a hybrid car gave me a picture of this. I was nervous and wondered if I could make the adjustments to this car while also navigating a new area. But, a day into the trip, I felt confident.

Tired and hungry, I pulled into a restaurant lot, parked, and pushed the lock on the key fob. Not hearing the familiar click, I tried again. I still didn't hear it but attributed this to my weariness. I went into the restaurant.

After a satisfying meal, I returned to the car and thought, *It's cold in here . . . It almost feels like the air conditioning is running.*

I looked at the console screen. The AC *was* running.

How can that be? I wondered. At the same moment, it hit me—I had never pushed the power button to turn the car off. I had only pushed the park button. No wonder the lock hadn't worked.

Recognition morphed into alarm. I looked around. Alarm gave way to gratitude, as I realized that no one had stolen the running car or my two computers, briefcase, and clothes, which were all unsecured. Embarrassed but thankful, I drove to my Airbnb.

When we first married, I was nervous and anxious: everything was so new. Could I really be the wife Jerry needed? Over time we developed our rhythm; a comfortable pattern of how we interact, communicate, make decisions, work, and relax together. I felt, *I've got this marriage thing down.*

But, precisely when I think that, my guard drops, just as it did after a short time with the unfamiliar car. And then we have one of *those* conversations. My confidence and understanding vanish. I wonder how we could have been married for over twenty years and still not understand each other. Or how it had taken me this long to figure something out.

When those thoughts return, I'm reminded to step back, thank God for my husband and our marriage, and tune my attention to the relational details that carry such big consequences. We may not recognize that we're continually adjusting, but adjustment is one constant in life and marriage.

IT'S JUST A PIECE OF PIE

I love coconut. Jerry doesn't. Coconut cakes and pies had been a frequent dessert in my childhood home. Since marrying, however, I don't make them unless I can share them with others.

Two years into our marriage, we lived near a restaurant famous for its variety of pies. One night the two of us went out just for dessert. I nearly drooled, envisioning the coconut cream pie piled high with whipped cream beside a steaming cup of coffee.

Before being seated, we learned that they had sold out of all the coconut cream pies. Nothing else even remotely sounded good, and I wanted to leave.

Jerry asked me if it would be okay if he ordered a piece of pie to go. Honestly, I couldn't believe he had the gall to ask that after my hopes had been so cruelly dashed. Not wanting to make a scene, I said, "Fine."

We were barely back in the van with his to-go bag when my eyes filled with tears. I choked out the words, "I can't believe you ordered pie."

"But I asked you and you said it was okay."

Confused, but wanting to please his wife, he offered to drive me to every restaurant in our county (he remembers saying the entire coast) in pursuit of coconut cream pie. But it was too late for me. The moment had passed.

Today, when speaking about marriage and communication, Jerry will say, "I can make my wife cry by just ordering a piece of pie."

In the scheme of life, a piece of pie, even coconut cream, is not worth the drama. But it serves a greater purpose than to add calories to my dietary intake. It reminds us that there is so much more to communication than words. I wanted Jerry to know what I was thinking and feeling without my saying it. That was an unfair expectation, whether married two years or twenty years.

MALE-FEMALE COMMUNICATION STYLES

Our friends were due to have a baby any day. When Jerry got off the phone with one of the guys in his small group, he told me the baby had been born and that everyone was healthy. I asked whether they'd had a boy or a girl. He replied, "I don't know. It's a baby."

To him, that was sufficient information. He quickly learned, though, that women, at least his woman, want all the details: gender, weight, length, how long the labor was, and the baby's name.

He has worked hard since then to gather information to satisfy his I-want-the-details wife. His preferred solution would be for babies to come with their own baseball card with the stats on their back. Our communication styles remain a work in progress.

"I had a bad day today," Jerry commented one day after work.

Wanting to be a supportive and caring wife, I asked, "Do you want to talk about it?"

"I just did."

That was all he needed or wanted to say. He was proud that he could articulate that much, whereas I wanted to know what had happened, hour by hour. Thankfully, God had been teaching me about the differences in our personalities, allowing me to give him space rather than increase his frustration by hounding him with questions.

I marvel at the intentional differences God engineered in men and women. Not just physically, but in terms of how we each process, our use of language, what we store as memories, and how we approach tasks or problem solve. Sometimes my marveling takes the form of, *What were you thinking, God?* At other times it contains gratitude for our different perspectives.

On the days when I rail against the way my husband does or doesn't function, I try to remember that I am taking issue with the Creator, the very One who announced that his creation of man and woman is very good. Jerry and I imagine God saying "This will be fun to watch" and then enjoying a belly laugh as he sees us learning to become one.

EMBRACING ADJUSTMENTS

1. The ways in which disability affects marriage aren't always as they seem. We are real people who struggle with genuine issues of life that often have nothing to do with disability. Celebrate normalcy where you can.
2. How do you keep from falling into the "I've got this" mentality in marriage? In what areas is God asking you to step back and fine-tune your relationship?
3. Is there a relationship adjustment you need to make? Have you ever talked about it? If not, make a plan to do so.

EMBRACING YOUR FRIENDS

1. If disability does not affect your life, don't let fear or discomfort prevent you from developing a friendship with a couple for whom disability is a factor. If you can push past your reservations, you will find that you as a couple are more alike than you are different.
2. Share stories of your marriage with your friends. Don't think they won't relate because you don't live with disability. It may help to hear that others have similar struggles.

PROVERBS 3:5

"Trust in the Lord with all your heart; do not depend on your own understanding."

PRAYER

Father God, thank you for our heritages, our families, and our backgrounds. They provide the foundation for our marriage. Remind us, though, that you are the unchanging rock. Bring us back to you when we feel our life to be full of misunderstandings and changes. Amen.

SIX

THE TYPICAL SPOUSE

"That is ridiculous. Don't they know the Americans with Disabilities Act? They will soon."

We were married just a few weeks when I uttered these words to my husband with all the ferocity I could muster. We had come upon a retail business that required one to step up to enter. I felt appalled at the lack of accessibility we had encountered. Jerry calmed me down and welcomed me, once again, into his world.

Though I had worked with people living in group homes and community settings for many years, disability became personal when it involved my husband. I discovered several personas I cycled through as I wrestled with this addition to my life. I still fall into some of these when I am not careful. See if you relate to any of these.

MAMA/PAPA BEAR

When you think of a mama bear with her cubs, what comes to mind? Fierce protector—at all costs. A defender, whether the perceived danger is real or assumed. That's what I was when I made the above statement. I was ready to go hunting in the name of justice. The cost didn't matter to me; I was going in for the kill. I was going to protect my husband (who had never asked me to), and the world of people with disabilities.

Mama and papa bears don't always take the time to gather or assess the correct information. If they see you before you see them, they believe you are coming for their cubs, even if you're simply on a hike. They quickly enter attack mode.

The problem with mama or papa bears in a marriage setting is this: you're not your spouse's mama or papa. They already have (or had) one of each and don't need, or likely wish for, another. By reacting fiercely, often without all the facts, we perpetuate the notion that people with disabilities can't think, speak, or act on their own behalf. We may thereby create more problems than we solve. We may strip our spouse of their dignity by acting on their behalf without first engaging in conversation. We may exhaust ourselves fighting a battle that isn't ours to fight.

AVENGER

While a mama bear protects, an avenger spouse has a superhero complex. They vow to right all the wrongs in the world, particularly those that affect their loved one. They subconsciously think, *It would be so much better if I had come into your life sooner.* They may forget that their campaign began with the person they love. Soon victory trumps relationship. They become warriors who take up the battle for other people, perhaps to the detriment of their own spouse, family, and self. An avenger may be so busy fighting battles for everyone else, and relishing the stroke to their own egos, that they forget about their partner and themself. Once you and your community view you as a disability avenger, it becomes difficult or you to be real. After all, avengers don't ask for assistance or even admit they may need help.

SMOTHERER

The smothering spouse isn't looking to save the day for the world but to take care of every—and I mean *every*—perceived need that exists in their family. Their actions tell their partner that it is doubtful he/she can do much on their own. Expectations are low for their spouse with a disability and are all consuming for themself. Initially, their motivation is to improve the quality of life for their loved one. But somewhere in the journey they determine that their own worth and value rests in being a caregiver. Even if they want to stop smothering, they can't because this has become their identity, their source of self-esteem.

The smothering spouse doesn't just handle the details for a particular instance, such as when their spouse is ill or traveling for business. Rather, it becomes their way of life. This has the potential to strip the spouse of the independence and skill they may have fought long and hard to gain. I remember the day Jerry reminded me that he had lived independently for ten years before I came into his life. Periodically, I still need that reminder.

When our actions imply that our spouse needs someone to take care of every detail, we hinder possibilities for our partner. Others may not see their potential as an employee, coworker, teacher, or candidate for a leadership position in the community or church.

The smotherer unduly pressures themselves with out-of-focus care. They need to handle everything and can never make a mistake, get sick, or take a break. No one else can help because they wouldn't do it right. They live in a state of constant exhaustion.

BEGRUDGING

The begrudging spouse has had enough. This disability gig might have been okay for a time, when getting closer parking spots was a perk. But the novelty has worn off, and the reality of *every day* has sunk in deeply. They resent the way disability has affected their life and marriage. It can become "all about me." This sets up an antagonistic relationship between the couple, shattering earlier dreams.

Begrudging spouses show frequent irritation, "Can't you do that any faster?" "Why do I always have to be the one to pick up something you drop?" "I married you to be your husband/wife, not your caregiver." Their loved one may hear these comments as a direct attack on their character and worth.

Those married to a begrudging spouse live on guard. They wonder when their husband/wife is going to have had enough and leave. Will they find someone else to marry who is less needy? They may even believe their disability reduces their value.

Closely related to the begrudging spouse is the one who plays the blame game. "Why did this happen to me/you/us? What did I/you/we do wrong? I'm trapped." They may even resent their spouse because life with disability is so much easier, or so it seems, while they are a living martyr, sacrificing everything.

DRILL SERGEANT

"Have you done your therapy exercises yet today? Did you remember to walk the dog twice while I was at work? Didn't you see the list on the kitchen counter of things you had to do today?" The drill sergeant spouse runs a tight operation and lives as though no one else will know what to do, when to do it, or how to do it unless he or she enlightens them. Because task accomplishment is so critical to this person, they treat their partner as something else to *do*, or as a tool used to get things done.

Do you recall the old show *Gomer Pyle: U.S.M.C.*? Gomer's drill sergeant was Sergeant Carter. Gomer wanted to be his friend but exasperated Sergeant Carter when he wouldn't follow established protocol. Sarge's role was to break Gomer until he understood and lived life by the rules of the Marines.

Drill sergeant partners may not be explicit in their words, but they want life on their terms. The sooner their spouse and everyone else gets on board with that, the happier they will all be, . . . or so they think.

ANONYMOUS SPOUSE

We know the anonymous spouse as "Jerry's wife" or "Margie's husband." The well spouse takes a back seat to the star of the show, the person with the disability. This may be either intentional or unplanned, but the pain is real.

I responded to an announcement made at church requesting meal help for a family in crisis. After the service, I found the coordinator. When I told her I would help, she thanked me and asked my name. *"Really? I've spoken to you several times and considered us to be growing friends."* These were the words running through my head. It wasn't until I identified myself as Jerry's wife that she made the connection.

Other people strive to create a persona of anonymity. That's not in itself a bad thing, but it could become problematic if this has become their sole source of identity and value. Or if they hold it over the head of their partner. "I never completed my degree or worked outside the home because I gave up everything to take care of you. No one even knows I exist."

Anonymity often comes with a "Woe is me" attitude when thoughts multiply about how hard our life is.

SUITABLE

When Adam needed companionship, God made a help meet *suitable* for him (Genesis 2:18). While the Scripture references the creation of Eve, the general principle carries over to all husbands and wives. Through marriage, God puts couples together for partnership, fellowship, intimacy, and procreation. The suitable partner understands that we're in this together. Doing life together means that communication flows freely, that both clarify assumptions and enjoy a free flow of forgiveness and grace. Being suitable means that we see our partner first as our husband or wife, rather than as a person who needs me or my help. A suitable spouse shuns comparisons and celebrates their spouse and relationship.

"Suitable" is a tension breaker in our home. When I've done something silly, or we're rebuilding from a time of forgiveness, I look at Jerry and say, "Remember, I'm suitable for you—God said so."

EMBRACING ROLES

1. Take some time to review these seven roles caregiving spouses may take on. In which persona, if any of these, do you spend most of your time? Are you satisfied there? Once you've made your determination, ask your spouse the same question.
2. What is one step you can take this week to become a more suitable spouse for your partner?
3. If you are the one with a disability, are there areas in your daily life you've allowed your spouse to pick up because this is easier for you? Is there anything you can change as you balance your time, responsibilities, and roles? Ask your spouse for their thoughts.

EMBRACING YOUR FRIENDS

1. If you notice unhealthy roles in your friends' marriage, pray about it.
2. Avoid putting your friend on a pedestal with "I could never do that; you are so very special."
3. Make room to listen to your friend—really listen, especially if disability entered your friend's life after they were married. You don't need answers. Listening without judgment goes a long way.

GENESIS 2:18

"The LORD God said, 'It is not good for the man to be alone. I will make a helper suitable for him.'"

PRAYER

Heavenly Father, thank you for being my caregiver. Thank you for showing me how to love. As I embrace your love and care more and more, please mold me to be the suitable mate my husband/wife needs. Thank you. We are on this journey together. Amen.

SEVEN

THE CAREGIVING SPOUSE

Caring for a loved one, especially a spouse newly affected by disability or chronic illness, is hard. Let's admit that from the start. Some believe that those who accept caregiving in their relationship at the outset don't succumb to the stresses and challenges experienced by those who've had the caregiving role thrust upon them. This is simply not true. You may have pledged "in sickness and in health" without ever considering what "sickness" might entail. Or perhaps you saw the question as multiple choice and subconsciously chose health over sickness.

Caregiver Stress Syndrome is a condition characterized by physical, mental, and emotional exhaustion. It typically results from a person neglecting their own physical and emotional health to focus on caring for an ill, injured, or disabled loved one.[14]

According to a report from the National Consensus Development Conference on Caregiving, the most common psychological symptoms of caregiver syndrome are depression, anxiety, and anger.[15] Another doctor suggests that the physical symptoms resulting from the exhausted caregivers' stress hormone levels are similar to those of individuals having post-traumatic stress disorder.[16] That's no surprise to caregivers. If they had only asked us, we could have saved them thousands of dollars in research and time spent traveling to conferences.

I've talked with hundreds of caregivers over the years. Many of us experience common symptoms. These include anxiety, loss of joy, exhaustion, lack of emotions or emotional control, impatience, hopelessness, headaches, changes in eating habits, or other physical ailments. Several years ago these came together for me as a perfect storm. We still refer to that day as "the Crash."

Jerry and I had been through a couple of long months, filled with commitments. We were moving toward the end of the year, which was a high demand time in our ministry. And it had been months since I'd taken a break from my role as Jerry's full-time caregiver.

Saturday was our ministry's Caregiver Day of Pampering, an annual event. Preparing for it and interacting with the ladies who attended had drained much of my emotional strength. Most years Jerry attended in the background to lend a hand where needed. This year he was representing the ministry at a national conference a few states away. At home, my mother was in her ninth year of living with us. She didn't need physical care but looked forward to us being home to talk with her and offer companionship. I wanted that, too, but didn't always have the stamina necessary.

We woke early the next day, Sunday. Jerry had arrived home in the wee hours of the night, and Mom was leaving early that morning to travel with my sister. I rose long enough to see them off and crawled back into bed. Almost immediately, I wept. Soon my tears became full-body sobs.

Jerry, still in bed, gently asked, "Honey, what's going on?"

As I was unable to articulate, he held me.

I was done.

I had exhausted all my social, emotional, mental, physical, and even spiritual reserves—I was empty, with nothing left to help myself or anyone else.

With deep compassion, and probably a little fear and trepidation, he calmly said, "It will be okay, sweetheart. We'll get through this together."

That was the final straw. The last tiny piece of my emotional dam broke, and I replied in a snarky tone through tears, "Sure. That's easy for you to say because you know that eventually I'll get up and get you dressed and in your chair. But who's going to take care of me?"

While Jerry wanted to assure me that he would, he knew not to say *those* words at *that* moment. He remained quiet. Later on, he told me that he had thought, "Oh no, she's right."

A short time later, I rose silently to get him up and dressed.

He asked, "What would you like for lunch?"

I made it clear that I didn't care. He could figure it out as I went back to bed. I rolled over to cry and sleep some more.

Donning his coat, Jerry went out to his van, ready to forage for food. The van has one front seat, mounted on a wheeled base. We can lock it to the passenger side for me when Jerry is behind the wheel, or to the driver's side when I or a friend drives. As Jerry and his friend had just returned overnight, the driver's seat remained in the van, preventing Jerry from driving. Because of their late arrival, he had told his friend who drove not to worry:

"Joan can change the seat out in the morning."

But this was *that morning*. He *was not* about to come back and ask me to move the seat.

He checked his wallet but didn't have enough money to order delivery. These were pre-Venmo and Cash App days. After considering his options, he determined to roll his chair to the nearby Wawa, where he could get cash and food. For those not blessed to live near a Wawa, it's the best convenience store in the country.

The mile distance entailed the need to navigate cracked and uneven sidewalks and a take-your-breath-away-if-walking steep hill. The forty minutes it took gave him ample time to consider what to buy.

He filled the bags as full as he could carry with sandwiches, salty treats, sweet surprises, and other things he thought I might enjoy. Then he rolled home and cautiously entered our room.

Still asleep, I didn't know he'd been gone for an hour and a half.

He approached the bed almost as though he were approaching a den of lions—which wasn't unreasonable, given my earlier reactions, and tossed the bags of food on the bed. "You can have any or all of this. If there's anything left, I'll eat that or figure out another plan."

Protein, salt, and sweets have never tasted as good as they did that day.

Jerry's effort to love me by holding me and offering soothing words of comfort had fallen short of my need for him to show me his love by his actions. But the time and energy he had put into the journey to purchase food spoke volumes to my exhausted spirit.

PLANNING FOR BURNOUT

I'm happy to say that I haven't had another crash like that since. Yet even the savviest caregiver may get caught off guard or be blindsided by burnout. How can we prepare for it before it happens?

Days after my tummy was full, my sleep reserves were replenished, and I was able to process things cognitively and emotionally, Jerry and I talked. We made a commitment to schedule differently, allowing for downtime after large events or travel. We now book a couple of free days into our calendar after such times. This reduces our guilt when we sleep in or spend a day doing nothing of value, because that's the purpose of those days.

I've learned to listen and accept Jerry's wisdom when he lovingly points out a stressful trend building. I can't always see the signs in the same way he does.

We no longer allow ourselves to be without an emergency stash of cash (pre-Venmo or Cash App days) for times we might need to order in or ask a friend to pick up something for us. Jerry encourages me to call a friend, go out to lunch, take a bike ride, or enjoy a nap in my hammock.

When he can, my hubby asks if I have the time to assist with something, rather than assuming or expecting me to help. When I think of it, I will suggest that Jerry ask a friend he is driving with to fill up the gas tank before they get home.

SELF-CARE

When we plan and build in margin, we are well on the way to a healthier life for me as a caregiver. But it's the unexpected events—the day when the van battery is dead or the joystick on the wheelchair falls off or that nagging skin breakdown reopens after months of doggedly pursuing healing that catches me off guard.

Inevitably, that's when a well-meaning friend offers in a singsong voice, "Remember, it is important for you to take care of yourself." I understand the heart behind their comment. But it can feel disingenuous because the person who shared may not truly understand my situation.

How should a caregiving spouse look at self-care? Many suggest that it might involve a massage, time away, or indulgence in a special treat. I'm all for those ideas; however, many of us can't afford these perks, either in terms of time or of money. Following are some no cost ideas from a fellow caregiving spouse.

Life wouldn't be so hard if we didn't expect it to be so easy.

We learned this on our first anniversary when we attended a Family Life Marriage conference, and it has been an important principle we refer to often. I don't like being told to set realistic expectations. I'm not sure I know what is realistic, but this I know to be true: life will be hard. Jesus reminds us of this in John 16:33: "In this world you will have trouble . . ." Acknowledging and expecting hard times changes the direction of my downward-spiraling thoughts.

There is a fine line between caring for our loved one and caring for ourself.

The airlines, when giving safety instructions, tell passengers to put on their own oxygen mask first before helping others. By masking yourself, you ensure your ability to care for others. This is easier to understand for an in-flight emergency than it is for day-to-day life on the ground.

Sometimes my mask is as simple as asking Jerry, when he calls for help, if he can wait for me to finish what I'm involved in. If he can, I wrap up my lunch, the chapter I'm reading, or the floor I'm mopping. If I take a little longer than expected, I let him know I haven't forgotten him. He knows that, ultimately, I'll take better care of him if I take a few minutes to complete what currently has my attention.

The challenge is tougher when the person you care for can't process a delay and may continue to call out for you. If it doesn't endanger your loved one, it may still be of benefit for you to complete what you're doing before responding. This wouldn't qualify as neglect if it's time limited. It's self-care.

Balance

Self-care and caregiving require balance. Perhaps I can juggle five balls (tasks) today. But there are seven demanding my attention. I must choose which ones I'll intentionally pick up. I leave the other two, knowing I can effectively work with the five in my hands. Setting aside the extra two doesn't mean they aren't important, but I don't have to stretch myself to keep them all in the air. I can address them another day, or the next week when I set aside a different ball and pick up one I had left earlier.

You're Not Alone

One blessing of living today is the multiple ways by which we can connect with other caregivers. Text and messaging services, the internet, or community groups offer round-the-clock support.[17] Knowing we're not the only one facing the sometimes daunting task of caregiving in marriage is reassuring. Jill Case Brown wrote *We Are Stronger Than We Look* to bring the reality of life as a caregiver into the open. Her husband became a quadriplegic after they had married, and her honest sharing offers a sense of identity for caregivers and a quiet reassurance that we are not alone.

Learning tips and tricks from other caregiving spouses and having one another's backs can be a lifesaver. I have two girlfriends who are also caregiving wives. Interacting with them undergirds my sanity. We text each other day or night, often with few words; we all just get it. We pray, rejoice, cry, and laugh together. Their companionship, even though we don't live in the same town, is priceless.

Apples and Oranges

As you interact and talk with other caregivers, beware of comparing someone else's life with your own. You'll always come up short. Yes, we're all caregivers, but the specifics vary. Nearly every family caregiver I know points to another family and expresses thanks that they don't carry *that* burden. The funny thing is, the other caregiver often thinks the same thing about them. Be wary of wishing to trade away what you know for what you don't know.

One other comparison to guard against is the way our lives used to be, as opposed to the way they are now. Each life is constantly changing, in both pleasant and hard ways. In years to come, we may wish for these good ol' days.

Celebrate the little things with grace and humor.

We shout "Yahoo" when we have a day that doesn't require a wardrobe change. Getting the pile of laundry put away the same day it came out of the dryer may give cause for a cheer. The morning the van starts after it had a dead battery may ignite a happy dance in the driveway. This chapter for me opened by my admission that life is hard. That's true, but life is also a joy. Acknowledge the seemingly insignificant things. The lift you'll feel may surprise you.

Faith reminds us that there is more.
Remember John 16:33, in which Jesus acknowledged that there will always be trouble in this world? That clause is just part of the verse. Here is the whole statement: "'I have told you these things, so that in me you may have peace. In this world, you will have trouble. But take heart. I have overcome the world.'"

Jesus is speaking to his followers, reminding them of his instructions in the preceding chapters. But look at this promise.

Take heart. Jesus has overcome. This world is not all there is.

God is molding and making me more like himself through my role as a caregiving wife. And he is doing the same for you.

There will come a day when I will no longer be a caregiver. There will also be a day when my husband won't need care. On that day, we'll fall at the feet of Jesus and worship him who has been the Caregiver to each of us throughout this life. So, journey on, knowing you are following in the steps of the One who gets it.

Mutual Caregiving

Yes, I am a caregiver. Most days I don't want to trade in that role. But to care well for my husband, I have to take responsibility to care for myself. Yet the blessing of a good relationship built on mutual respect means that the one I love and care for also cares for me—provided I let him.

Jerry's caregiving doesn't look the same as mine. He doesn't put me to bed each night or assist me in the shower. But there are many ways in which he cares for me, if I will only pay attention. He checks on me when he knows I have faced a tough situation or phone call; he thanks me for the ways I help him; he prays with me when I share a concern; he tunes in to my aches and pains and offers a foot rub, a back massage, or working on my arthritic thumbs. He is quick to say, "You've had enough on your plate for today. Let's order dinner out." He praises me to friends and family. He'll sit at the pool as my lifeguard while I swim laps. When he'd rather watch baseball, he'll offer to walk with me. He suggests that we watch a chick flick after days of sports as our steady television diet.

I hope you get the idea. I could write several more paragraphs on this, my favorite topic—Jerry. My point is to recognize his care and acknowledge how he gives back to me.

Health

Then came the day I had to focus on my health. For over a quarter of a century my life has revolved around giving Jerry the best care I could. I wanted him to be productive and live a full life. I allowed his medical care or needs to trump my own.

Until it caught up to me.

There came a time when thoughts of *I'll tend to that later* with regard to my own physical needs demanded I do so now. I could no longer ignore my body. Potential diagnoses were coming from my doctor. In my mouth, teeth were breaking. Having Jerry care for me wasn't enough.

I had to care for myself.

I found a dentist and scheduled an appointment. Fresh veggies and fruit became the basis of our grocery list. I've carved out time to exercise almost every day. The simple word *no* became more frequent in my vocabulary.

I didn't see an immediate change but had to trust I was doing the right things. I found a good example to follow. As we read in Joshua 3, the children of Israel finally crossed the Jordan River to take possession of the promised land. History tells us that the waters stopped flowing several miles upstream at a city called Adam. The people crossing the now dry Red Sea couldn't see the walls of water. They had to trust that God was acting on their behalf. He was—but he was operating several miles out of their line of sight.

Seek Replenishment from the Source.

Ted Cunningham shares in *Fun Loving You*:

> Underneath our kitchen sink, I keep a clear plastic jug. It's called the "Love Jug." When I pull the jug out, my kids scream, "No, not the Love Jug."
>
> I place the Love Jug on the counter and surround it with glasses of all different shapes and sizes. From the hose on the sink I fill up the jug and ask, "Who is the source?"
>
> The kids respond with, "God."
>
> "That's right. And our job is to connect to Him and allow Him to fill us every day. Then we go out and give our family, friends, and strangers the overflow," I say. As I pour from the jug into the individual glasses, the jug empties. Then I ask, "How do I replenish the water that I poured out? Do I wait for others to pour back into me?"
>
> "No, God refills you," my kids say.
>
> When you look to your loved one as the source of life, you automatically become dependent on him or her. Be sure your fulfillment comes from God.

EMBRACING CAREGIVING

1. When you hear the term *self-care*, what is your reaction? Which of the ideas offered in this chapter can you work on this week?
2. What is your source of fulfillment as a caregiving spouse? How does God refill you in the midst of your caregiving?
3. How can you, as the mate with a disability, increase your care for the one you love?

EMBRACING YOUR FRIENDS

1. Caregivers often speak in second person plural because our identity is so intertwined with that of our partner. If you notice this in another caregiver, gently help your friend recognize or develop their own voice.
2. What is one thing you can do to encourage a caregiving friend this week?
3. Offer to sit at your friend's house while he or she takes a nap so you can be available to their spouse if needed for thirty minutes or an hour.

MATTHEW 11:28–30

"'Come to me, all who labor and are heavy laden, and I will give you rest. Take my yoke upon you, and learn from me, for I am gentle and lowly in heart, and you will find rest for your souls. For my yoke is easy, and my burden is light.'"

PRAYER

Papa God, teach me to come to you for rest. Show me what it means to be yoked with you and to learn your rhythms of grace. Amen.

EIGHT

FAMILY AND HOME

Family. Those who grow up without one may dream of a loving family, but many in a dysfunctional family want to separate themselves as early as possible. Children raised in a healthy family may take it for granted and assume that everyone else has had similar experiences. Whether your home was led by two parents, a single parent, a grandparent, or a foster parent or parents, you bring history, expectations, and emotional connections from there into your marriage.

FAMILY OF ORIGIN

In an earlier chapter, I shared how differently Jerry and I had grown up in terms of playing table games. It would be delightful if our only adjustments had been so simple or could have been completed after our first year together as husband and wife . . .

We found, though, that our families' differences continued in areas such as finances, home repairs, and the volume and method by which we settled disagreements. I remember that two silly differences arose in relation to food.

Our first home was across the street from a grocery store. While preparing dinner, I realized we were out of lettuce. Jerry offered to go across the street to buy some. Trying to make it easy for him rather than specifying butter lettuce, red leaf, or iceberg, I told him it didn't matter what kind he bought. I could work with any kind of lettuce. The bag felt heavy when he handed it to me. I tried to hide my surprise when I pulled out a head of cabbage. He didn't understand. While I changed my plans and made coleslaw, he told me his mom used it to make a garden or tossed salad and that he had thought cabbage was a type of lettuce.

When Jerry's siblings came to visit, they were astonished to see a variety of salad dressing bottles in the refrigerator door, all obviously in use. It was then that I learned that Mom Borton had a one-salad-dressing-open-at-a-time rule.

Discovering these types of quirks and differences adds to the fun of growing together. Other matters, especially disability related, would be better discussed in advance than tripped over.

FAMILY CAREGIVING

For many individuals with disabilities, their parents, grandparents, and siblings were the first caregivers in their lives. When a spouse joins the family, some of the original caregivers may expect to relinquish their duties, while others expect to continue as before. It's important to discuss how you'll engage with your individual families from now on. If relatives have been providing personal care, do you both want them to continue? Are you assuming that your spouse will become your primary caregiver? Does your spouse want to be your caregiver?

What happens when parents or other family members need care? I've heard this often from caregivers: "Once a caregiver, always a caregiver." There's an assumption that because I am a caregiver for my spouse or child, it will be easy for me to take responsibility for relatives from either side as they age and need care. Even if this expectation is unspoken among the rest of the family, the issue shouldn't be unspoken between yourself and your partner. Clarify expectations between the two of you so you can respond as a team when a need arises.

CHILDREN

The decision to have or not have children is one with which every couple needs to wrestle. If children were brought into the relationship, the obvious answer is yes. Wrestling with this question as a couple with disability adds a few more variables to consider. Whether or not the woman is the spouse with a disability, pregnancy and child rearing will affect their shared lives.

Jerry and I both enjoy children. As a single adult, I always assumed that, once married, I would have children. Even before we married, as we talked, we recognized that:

1. We were both in our later thirties. This is not too old to bear a child, but it will likely be more difficult than for younger people.
2. We wanted to have a couple years of "just us" as we adapted to marriage before we had kids. Having already made the decision that I'd help Jerry with his personal care, we talked about how that function might be affected as a pregnancy progressed or if we had a newborn. We had never heard of a newborn who slept soundly through the night, every night.

Practical realities were that I'd either need to get up to get Jerry up to tend to the baby overnight (okay, not practical), or I'd be the one to tend to all the baby's overnight needs.
3. Even if we became pregnant, we'd face eighteen years of child raising, plus college and potential additional challenges. Could we see our older selves parenting at each new level?

Our thought processes aren't prescriptive for every couple, but, ultimately, we chose to not have biological children. My sister's five kids had embraced me as their "other mother," so some of my maternal instincts were engaged. Only minutes after meeting Jerry, our nieces and nephews also embraced him. This may have had something to do with the rides they took with him on his chair.

We came quickly to our decision. But as the years progressed, I second-guess it more often than I did when we'd first made it. There is no guarantee if we'd had children, that they would have cared for us as we aged.

We've found, unexpectantly, that making friends is harder in our senior years without kids or grandkids. When we were all younger, our friends who were new parents welcomed us into their lives, in part to combat the isolation newborns or toddlers can bring. They wanted adult company. Now friends with grandchildren spend much of their time attending dance, music, and sporting events and have little time for friends who don't do the same.

Our second Thanksgiving found us at my parents' home, celebrating with them and my sister and her family, who were on a furlough from their mission field. One day Mom; my sister, Ginny; our ten-year-old niece; and Jerry and I were out. Our niece shared that she had a Christmas wish only Uncle Jerry and Aunt Joan could fulfill. We asked her what that was, and she gleefully replied, "Cousins." We all snickered. Jerry, recognizing that there were just four weeks until Christmas, told her not to get her hopes up. Her innocent reply, "Why, aren't you guys having any luck?" still lives in our family memory banks as though this exchange had taken place today.

You may arrive at a different decision than we did. That's fine. You may also have prayerfully arrived at your decision, only to be surprised later when you learned that there was a baby coming when you had been told there could never be one.

Though we chose not to have a child by birth, we found plenty of opportunities to be involved in the lives of children. Jerry and I opened our home to those in need. Sometimes we had children staying with us through a respite or foster care system. Sometimes we homed the teen son of friends whose parents needed a break. Because we worked in a field with children and youth in emergency situations, Jerry said he never knew who would be at the dinner table or in the guest room on any given night.

Offering a temporary home to children in crisis is difficult, but it provided a way for us to invest in the lives of children. It was difficult to let them go after a brief time, but this was what we believed God was asking us to do. They met our needs to nurture, and we met their needs for a safe place. God even blessed us with a young mom and her newborn for several weeks. What a delight to cuddle that infant and pray over him. I whispered into his tiny, perfectly formed ear about how much his heavenly Father loved him.

We had a season in which we volunteered together in the church toddler nursery. For the safety of everyone, Jerry stayed stationary against a wall and was the keeper of the snacks.

The little ones quickly became comfortable with someone in a wheelchair, or perhaps in their eyes a giant stroller. It was a positive experience for all of us.

Whatever decision you arrive at, own it. If it's the decision you and your spouse believe is God's best for you, there's no need to explain it to others, excuse it, or hide it.

HOME RESPONSIBILITIES

Handling the responsibilities of a home, whether you own, rent, or share, can be a struggle for all couples. As we've seen in many areas of life, disability may complicate this. One of the inevitable results of using a wheelchair is that tire tracks often decorate the tile floor. I can tell Jerry about them and make him feel uncomfortable moving around, or I can deal with them. We dealt with it by purchasing a robotic mop that we named Rosie.

Thinking about the floors brings to mind a story from the summer before we married. Jerry moved from Indiana to California, where I lived. The previous year I had purchased a small condo. One upgrade I had done was to replace all the carpet with a beautiful light gray option.

Shortly before Jerry arrived, a friend built a ramp to give him access to the front door, which had one step. After he moved in, another friend offered to paint it to preserve the wood. Jerry planned to stay inside all day, so before I went to work for the day I pulled the ramp away from the door. We asked our friend not to put it back; that way, when I came home from work, I'd be ensured that it was dry and could move it back.

In the mid-afternoon Jerry saw that our painter friends were gone and that the ramp had been put back in place. He assumed it had dried and rolled outside to get the mail. Not seeing any paint marks from his wheels on our cement patio, he felt safe to go back inside. As is his habit, he perused the mail while turning circles in his chair. After a couple of circles, he looked down. There on the new light gray carpet were dark brown concentric circles from the front door to a few feet into the living room.

He called me at the office, and his first words were, "Should I call the moving truck back?"

"What? Why would you ask that? What happened?"

As soon as he told me, I exclaimed, "Don't move. I'm coming home."

I hung up the phone and asked my coworkers how to get oil-based paint stains out of the carpet. I stopped by the drugstore and purchased dry cleaning fluid.

Armed with old towels, I asked him to roll on the rags until no more paint came off his wheels. Once his chair was clean, I spent the next several hours on the floor scrubbing paint out of the carpet. I know he felt worse than I did. His memories of that day are of uttering "I'm sorry" over and over again.

Varying perspectives on our home and its furnishings arose when we needed to replace our living room sofa. Never before having purchased furniture, Jerry was astonished by the price. He questioned whether we really needed a couch; after all, he would never use it. To him, this seemed like a colossal waste of hard-earned money.

Then there was the decision about the placement of furniture. As a doting bride, I wanted our home to be fully accessible for Jerry. Some places we lived were easily manageable for him. With others, we made do the best we could. Twice in our lives I've looked at Jerry and commented, "This home is so accessible for you it's become inaccessible to me."

I wasn't tripping over things or unable to move about, but the pendulum had swung in the opposite direction. I felt as though there were no designated spaces for me to store my things. It took some time, but he got it. We've tried since then to find common ground. Occasionally, there is something Jerry can't get to. But I'm happy and willing to assist, so the setup works for both of us.

Growing up, I wouldn't have called my dad handy, but I can't recall Mom and Dad ever hiring someone to come in and do a job. Dad painted the house both inside and out, and one summer he reroofed our home. He did a great job with the lawn and garden and small plumbing jobs. My dad, an industrial engineer, was attentive to details. He regularly walked through the home with a paintbrush and can of paint and touched up nicks or scars.

Jerry's dad was McGyver.[18] He could fix almost anything, but not necessarily so that it functioned or looked the same as it had before.

Our backgrounds influenced how we looked at home maintenance and repair. Jerry was well aware of the dings wheelchairs can cause. Marks, scratches, or unique ways to repair something were standard for him.

Although I'm not a neat freak, I felt that our home's appearance reflected negatively on me. When a nick occurred or paint was scratched, I wanted this corrected immediately. I didn't realize that my desire to keep a pleasant house for me and my husband (and maybe visiting parents) was creating for Jerry a feeling of living in a showpiece. He found it difficult to relax and feel at home.

When we finally talked this out, we both came away with a better understanding of why we each responded as we did. We agreed that:

- When the budget allows, we hire a house cleaner once or twice a month.
- Jerry's ability to feel at home in our home, which we both paid for, ranked higher than my need to have unblemished walls. I've lessened my focus on keeping everything pristine, and he tries to be mindful while moving around. If an opening is a tight fit and may not work for his passage, he asks for help instead of forging ahead.
- Jerry assumes responsibility for asking a friend to come over once every other month and go through the house to spackle and touch up paint.

We talk more now about bigger household projects, including replacing furniture or appliances and why we need them. What is the estimated cost? How and when do we need to budget for each?

We follow a similar pattern for vehicle maintenance. We own two cars, one that either of us can drive and the other that only I drive. He stays mindful of the need for and scheduling of routine maintenance. Either of us calls the mechanic and makes the plan.

Sometimes I feel bad that, with all the things Jerry needs to do and how slowly he moves through projects, oversight of maintenance is his responsibility. Then I realize that I now move more slowly too, both because of the ways I assist him and the extra things I take off his plate. And that's okay. Sharing the responsibility, whether 50/50 or 70/30 or by any other type of split, is appropriate. This is one way in which he serves me and dies to himself.

When we got married, I had a full-time job. Jerry left his own full-time job to move to California, where I lived and owned a small home. In the days of job searching, he also picked up extra chores around the house. I doubt I'll forget the time his mom called.

"What are you doing?"

"Dishes—I'm washing and Jerry's drying." In those days before video calls, we couldn't see her face, yet I knew from her tone that she couldn't believe I expected her son to help.

Jerry has never minded taking part in home tasks. He does mind, though, if I go back and redo the job. This realization became another opportunity for me to adjust my expectations and express gratitude that we can work together.

The condo we lived in when we were first married had a stackable washer and dryer. Little did I know when I bought it as a single person that it would be the perfect setup for my future hubby in a wheelchair. He could move loads between machines and take them out of the dryer when complete.

Today we divide chores differently than we used to. That's okay. Just because we do things one way for a time doesn't mean the pattern is set for life.

He may offer to take a task off my list, but will the extra time it requires of him be worth the tradeoff to save me a few minutes? Sometimes it is, but not always. Be willing to try new options. Alter and adjust. And forgive yourself and your spouse when you do it imperfectly.

EMBRACING FAMILY AND HOME

1. When is the last time you thanked God for the people who make up your extended family, otherwise known as in-laws? Even if they have some unusual quirks or drive you batty, remember that they raised the man or woman you love and joined your life to. They must have done something right.
2. If God blesses you with children, try to avoid using them in a caregiving or spousal role. If you don't have children, how can you invest in the lives of children outside the home?
3. When was the last time you and your honey sat down and talked about needs around the house and how to get them done? Is it time to look at this again?

EMBRACING YOUR FRIENDS

1. Don't assume that your friends can't have children. You can pray for their decision, but, as with any couple, don't pry. If they do have kids, offer a helping hand periodically.
2. If you or your friends complain about the in-laws, encourage them (and yourself) to focus on the positive traits.
3. Could you help your friends by taking a regular chore off their list? If you live nearby, perhaps you could take the trash cans to the curb each week. Or once a month stop in to change any light bulbs as needed or touch up paint.

PSALM 133:1

"How good and pleasant it is when God's people live together in unity!".

PRAYER

Lord, my spouse and I are on the same side. Remind us of that often. Help me focus more on my spouse's needs. Thank you for holding both of us in the palm of your hand. Amen.

NINE

ATTENDANT CARE

To have or not to have attendants? Sorry, Shakespeare, but this is my question. And it is one we may ask and answer in different ways throughout the course of our lives.

Oddly enough, Jerry and I didn't talk about the specifics of his care routine before we got married. I don't recommend this plan. I'm not sure why we left this important information unspoken, other than that we were both starry eyed. I had lived and worked with people with many kinds of disabilities, and I think we both assumed I knew what would be involved. In theory, I did.

Individuals' specific needs for help vary widely because of disability, time, accessibility, and more. Even though we never talked about the specifics of what personal care would look like, we decided initially that we wouldn't hire attendants. As newlyweds, we weren't ready to live our life on others' schedules. I wanted to assist Jerry with his care, saving him time in the morning and evening. And I did. He went from taking about four hours to get ready each morning to requiring less than two. While we factored in the time he'd save, however, we forgot to consider the time I'd lose. Again, my only defense is that we were starry eyed in love; I can't even attribute this to our being young.

Another outcome we hadn't thought through was Jerry's loss of independence. Prior to marriage, he had completed his own self-care. Though he gained time through my help, his ability to transfer from bed to his chair and back again without help vanished from lack of use.

When we informed some friends in similar situations that we were not using attendants, we were surprised at their reactions. They strongly expressed their feelings, telling us that, in their opinions, not using attendants was wrong. They cautioned against the undue stress we would be putting on our marriage. We considered their words, along with our personalities and lifestyle. They almost convinced me, but first I checked to see if the Bible offered direction. It did not. I knew that, if God didn't provide us with standards in this area, we could still fall back on freedom and grace. As with decisions about having children, each couple must wrestle with the variables and dynamics of their lives.

As with us, you'll find that your decisions change and morph with time and circumstance. That's expected. Understanding some blessings and challenges involved with having a personal care attendant (PCA) as a part of your life may aid in your decision making.

BENEFITS OF USING PCAS

- Attendants allow the spouse to keep their role as husband or wife separate from that of caregiver. It's difficult to change one's focus repeatedly from personal care to intimacy.

- The spouse may have more flexibility for self-care or to focus on family needs.
- In an emergency, there will be people you can call immediately who know how to step in if the caregiving spouse has to travel or becomes incapacitated.

CHALLENGES IN USING PCAS

- You'll have an unfamiliar person, perhaps a stranger at first, in your home and around your family members.
- Attendants have varying levels of reliability. You need a backup plan.
- Even the best attendants will rarely provide the same level of care a family member does.
- Many insurance programs will not pay for personal care help. Private pay can be prohibitive.
- There's less flexibility and spontaneity in schedule and activity when one needs to be home and ready for attendants as scheduled.

If, after evaluating your family's lifestyle and needs, you agree to engage attendants, consider these questions prior to recruiting:

- What are the specific needs that require help? How much time will they entail?
- Do you prefer male or female attendants? What is your mate's perspective on this?
- Which one of you will manage or oversee the attendant? Likely, this will be the partner needing care, as long as they are able.
- What interaction do you expect between the PCA and other family members in the home?

- Are you willing to work with someone whose primary language differs from yours?
- Are there any sources of financial aid available in your area for attendant care? Would it be wise to hire attendants if this requires the spouse to take on a job to cover the cost?
- Are there other duties you'd like the PCA to complete when they have down time on their shift? Be creative to most effectively use their time. After all, you don't want to pay for someone to sit and read a book just to meet the minimum hours. If, on the other hand, your family member or friend is voluntarily serving as a PCA, try not to overwhelm them with a "honey-do" list *unless they offer to help in this way.*

After you have made the broad decision to engage PCAs, you must determine if you'll handle the hiring (whether volunteer or paid) privately or work through an agency. If you choose to manage your PCAs privately, the answers to the following questions will help to shape your next steps:

- Will you seek volunteers or privately hire PCAs?
- Do you prefer someone you don't know in the interest of professional distance, or are you willing to hire friends/family who may learn more about your life than they otherwise would?
- How will you advertise? How will you manage the application process, background checks, and interviews?
- How will you determine an appropriate pay rate? Who will handle payroll and your responsibility for taxes?
- Do you need to consider any changes to your insurance required for having an in-home employee?

- In the event you need to fire an attendant, do you know how to do so? Is there a contingency plan to provide for the needed care if there's a gap between attendants?

For some, the business side of PCAs is best handled by contracting with an agency. This will cost more per hour, but the application, background checks, and financial details will be out of your hands. Before interviewing and selecting an agency, consider:

- Do you have a choice of which agency to work with, or is there only one in your area?
- Are you expected to recruit your own PCAs and then refer them to the agency for on-boarding?
- What information will the agency tell you about the candidate's background before you hire them?
- What is the minimum number of hours per shift the agency requires?
- Does the agency allow the PCA to perform other tasks when you do not directly need their help for the entire shift (e.g., while you are showering or toileting, can they do laundry, light cleanup, food prep, etc.)?

When Jerry was single, he used attendants only when he traveled for camps or other speaking engagements. He invited a friend to travel with and assist him, or he recruited in advance guys from a nearby college or church to help him at his destination.

As we have grown as a couple, our thoughts and desires about attendants have changed. And then came our first emergency. When my best friend's husband died in a workplace accident, she lived at the other end of the state. I wanted and needed to be there but couldn't leave my husband.

Jerry called the men in his small group at church. When he told them what had happened, they said, "Tell Joan to go. We'll take care of things here." And that's what we did. I walked through the first ten days of grief with my friend and her daughters, while Jerry's friends walked together through their first experience as personal care attendants. Talk about ways to deepen a friendship . . .

Since then, we use attendants periodically. When I need to travel for ministry or family needs, Jerry finds people to step in. To this point, twenty-seven years into marriage, we've never paid for personal care attendants. We've explored this option a few times, but the cost has been prohibitive. Perhaps better said, we have other priorities for our funds. Until I can no longer provide his care, I will.

Sometimes people reference the burden or challenge of caregiving. Most days I don't think like that. Our routine is built into our lives; it's just the way we function. We've learned the ebbs and flows of time, helping us to determine when I need to be helping and when I can run an errand or take a walk and be back in thirty minutes before he needs me again.

Caregiving is not a burden. It's a choice I make repeatedly to love my husband by helping him. Lest you join the scores of people who say how lucky Jerry is to have me, let me assure you, again, that caregiving is *not* a one-way street. Especially caregiving in marriage. Jerry cares for me each day, too. Whether by remembering to clean up his breakfast tray, carrying my plate to the sink after dinner, calling for someone to tend to minor house projects, or giving me a foot rub most nights, he gives back and cares for me.

Each time we move to a new city, we have to build rapport and invite new people into this very private part of our lives. In one state, I unexpectedly went to the hospital with an infection.

Again, Jerry called the men he fellowshipped with at church, and they put together a schedule and came to his rescue. But here's the most amazing part of that unplanned journey: some of those guys said, "Joan does this every day, all the time? I could continue doing this on Tuesday mornings or Thursday evenings."

And so began several years of having attendants three mornings and three evenings a week. All volunteers. One of them even recruited another guy from church to join the team. Still others said, "I can't commit to every week, but if Joan needs to go away or is sick, I'll be there."

And they were.

Looking back, Jerry realizes that these guys were his closest friends. When someone comes at the crack of dawn and assists with intimate care, the two quickly become close. For a time I was jealous he had so much time with friends. I lacked a similar amount of girlfriend time.

These relationships wouldn't have happened with a paid attendant who maintained detached professionalism. Not that you should expect your small group to respond in the same way. But one has to have the courage to ask. And they need the courage to answer.

I'm sometimes asked if it's weird to have another man in my bedroom. Initially, I felt a little self-conscious, but I learned to keep a robe by my bedside so that, if I needed to get up while they were present, I could do so without embarrassment.

For some guys, especially when they were new and learning the ropes, I got up early and went out to the living room. I had my coffee and read while they helped Jerry. This gave them the flexibility to learn without worrying about disturbing me. It also helped me to keep my mouth shut.

Over time I became so comfortable with the friends who came in and went out that I continued to sleep. Yes, on the other side of the bed from which they were assisting Jerry. Call it exhaustion or a blessing from God or both. Sometimes I would wake up surprised to see Jerry already in his chair. I had never heard the guys coming and going.

Admittedly, some of my sleep was light. The PCA might ask Jerry where to find some item they had run out of. If Jerry was unsure, I'd mumble, "right side of the closet, third shelf down," and then blissfully resume my gentle snoring. I don't know how I did that. I hadn't been aware I was awake, but this happened more than once.

Jerry comments, "No one will ever care for me the way Joan does." This is true. But many can come close if given the opportunity to learn. My biggest challenge was to let go. If I continually interject tips or ways to do things, these caregivers may feel as though they'll never measure up. Jerry's biggest challenge: "Being willing to ask my friends. That's hard."

Perhaps you, as the spouse-caregiver, need to be the one to explain to attendants the steps involved in the routine. Beware of what I call the "CS Affect," so named for a friend who was also a caregiving wife. We attended church together. Periodically she would comment, "I don't understand why the men will help Jerry and not my husband."

This seemed odd to us because we knew they were both well loved by the church members. We explored this and learned the reason. She was exacting. Her career choice and personality fit her precise way of doing things. Anyone who stood in for her needed to do everything in the same way, or she'd point out any area of deviance. These men who volunteered to serve their friend and God didn't have the same training or experience and sometimes missed a step. The guys who tried to help told us they feared they'd never be good enough to satisfy her, even though her husband would have been safe and well cared for.

Jerry made the time with a PCA fun. They talked, laughed, and enjoyed great fellowship. Did they do everything the way I would? Absolutely not. But Jerry is healthy, ready for the day, and presentable. Only once were his shoes put on the wrong feet. I've learned to let go of some of my expectations. Jerry has learned to let me make one final tweak before he rolls out the door.

If you have the option, start with whatever is "easier." Jerry's evening routine involves much less care and time than his morning routine. We found it preferable to start with a new person in the evening. As comfort levels develop, you can then explore the possibility of morning help.

Alex, a friend who, in our early years, helped with some of Jerry's care, welcomed me home from a business trip. He related his favorite Jerry-care story. Alex was one of three guys who were at our home, helping Jerry with his morning routine. Often when one of the guys was new, they would tag team a shift to demonstrate how everything would work. At one point Jerry said, "Hey, thanks a lot. I know some guys wouldn't be comfortable dressing another guy."

Alex jumped in with, "I know. I'm one of them." Alex tells me that everyone laughed . . . and they moved on. While it was uncomfortable, Alex shared that he had experienced the body of Christ in action.

Today, though Alex can no longer help because of his own health needs, he prays for us regularly, especially when I am away, that I will return safely. I'll take that.

Thank your personal care attendants, whether paid, family members, or volunteers. You know how critical their work is. Be sure they hear from you often of your gratitude and appreciation. For many, those words of encouragement will go further than any numbers written on a paycheck. And an occasional gift card for coffee or fuel doesn't hurt, either.

EMBRACING ATTENDANTS
1. It's helpful to hear how others manage attendants and daily life. But remember, there's no single standard, right or wrong, answer. This is a decision about what works for you and your family.
2. If you are a caregiving spouse, check your expectations. Your spouse needs to be safe and healthy, but no one else will ever care in precisely the same way you do.
3. Be creative. Perhaps using attendants on certain days would be beneficial, but you can't afford them seven days a week. A hybrid model may be for you.

EMBRACING YOUR FRIENDS
1. So, you've never dressed an adult before. It doesn't take an advanced degree. Offer to learn how you can assist, even periodically, in the care routine of a friend with a disability.
2. Pay attention if you hear of a retreat or other activity the caregiving spouse may want to attend. Ask how you might encourage or support them to do so.
3. If personal care isn't your thing (and it's not for everyone), how else can you come alongside a caregiving spouse and lighten their load? Is it raking leaves or shoveling snow? Providing a meal periodically? Meeting them for coffee or lunch? Praying for them?

JOHN 15:12-13
"'My command is this: Love each other as I have loved you. Greater love has no one than this, to lay down one's life for one's friends.'"

PRAYER

Thank you, God, for the variety and freedom of choice we have in life. Thank you for those who have made it their life work to care for others. Would you bless and encourage PCAs, both volunteer and paid? Please raise up others to come alongside those who need additional care. Show my partner and me how we can manage personal care needs. Amen.

TEN

TRAVEL

"He was born with a suitcase in his hand." Jerry's mom made that statement to me in the early years of our relationship. More proof that he and I belong together: we both enjoy travel.

Others marvel at our volume of travel. Other families affected by disability frequently ask, "How do you do that?" or comment "I'd be afraid to travel with my spouse and their wheelchair."

There are risks, but every day we face a world of risk. Each person must evaluate the level at which they are willing to engage. The tradeoff is exploring new areas, visiting beloved family and friends, or taking part in a meaningful conference or event.

If you are ready for adventure, the following tips and tricks will make your trips as hassle free as possible.

PLANNING

Before you get too far along in your dreams, there are some decisions you must make to set the parameters, whether for business or pleasure. For example, will both of you go or only one? What are the pros and cons of each?

We prefer to travel together but will go solo if a need warrants. I appreciate those times when Jerry looks at me and says, "It's time for you to schedule some time away." I know it's difficult for him to have a few days alone. He tells me that he loves the first evening when he chooses what to eat, what to watch on TV, and how to spend his time. But by the second day the fun fades.

When he gifts me with the opportunity to go away, I travel with confidence, assured that he can manage. In preparation, Jerry schedules attendants. I make his time more efficient by putting together the clothes he'll need each day, based on his schedule of meetings (outfits, if you will, though I'm told that men don't wear outfits). His attendants don't have to match colors; they simply choose what's on the hanger closest to the door.

Likewise, there are times he needs to travel for a speaking engagement, a meeting, or even the fun of baseball. I always get the first right of refusal for the trip; we've found that occasionally we benefit from a brief break. Most often he will seek a guy friend who will travel with him and assist with attendant care and travel needs.

PACKING

One of the best things we ever did was to create a standard packing list. This includes everything we might take along for a trip to any climate or venue, broken down by category (clothes, toiletries, medications, equipment, and so on). Prior to travel I print it out and cross off things not needed for this journey. As I pack, each item gets checked off.

We cannot pack certain articles until the morning we leave. I highlight those boxes and put the list on top of the suitcase. Those items are the last things I gather prior to departing. Because we travel frequently, we keep duplicates of our most needed supplies. We keep one bag always packed with the most critical supplies to ensure that we'll leave nothing behind.

EQUIPMENT OR ATTENDANTS

In our early years of marriage, we traveled with very little equipment. We had a routine. We knew that, with a slide board and gait belt, we could handle any transfer. Until one night. I got into position to transfer my husband to the hotel bed, and my knee refused to join the party. We were in a city where we didn't know anyone. To this day I can't tell you how he got into bed that night or up the next morning. God must have sent angels. I know, though, that we fell asleep knowing we had just crossed a new threshold.

Now we travel with either more equipment or an attendant or both. Our destination and transportation determine which method we use. If we attend a conference or are in an area where we know other people, we'll ask some guys if one could help us with transfers each morning and evening. They are usually more than willing to assist if we just ask. That brief period of help is all we need to keep both our bodies safe. It also gives our friends a glimpse into our life.

This is the way my dad first got to know his future-son-in-law. Before we began dating, Jerry and I both stayed after the conference for different reasons. Jerry had hired a local college student to be his attendant, and my parents were visiting me. Early one morning the phone in my hotel room rang. It was Jerry, asking if my dad would help him get up that morning. The attendant had called out sick, and Jerry knew no one else. It pleased me when my dad said he would.

I still laugh at my dad's statement when he met up with Mom and me again: "That boy needs new socks. He has holes all over his." What Dad didn't understand was that the dressing stick Jerry used when at home pulled his socks up only by hooking into the knitting.

On a recent trip we stayed with friends who also live with disability. This was a breath of fresh air for us at the end of a four-week trip. Our friends set up the rooms, knowing how we would need to use them. They worked out a schedule for times when Jerry could use their roll-in shower without their needing it.

Traveling to places where we don't have connections means that we take or rent equipment. If we're driving, we take a portable electric lift with us, along with a backup battery. Other equipment we pack includes a rolling shower chair, a slide board, a gait belt, and a transfer ladder. We may not use them all, but having them provides options.

A side note here: packing the van can be a bit like a game of Jenga—trying as we do to figure out which piece will fit or move without disrupting all the others. I don't have enough hands or the strength to load and unload the van well. Jerry arranges with a neighbor or family member nearby to meet at a designated time to load and unload the vehicle. Even strangers in the hotel's parking lot will help if we just ask. Engaging helping hands before we even hit the road means that Jerry and I start the trip with better attitudes.

When flying or cruising, we find it easier to rent equipment and have it delivered to our destination or ship. Cruising makes this very easy (though we haven't cruised post-Covid). There are medical equipment providers who specialize in equipment for cruises, and cruise lines keep a list of preferred providers. What a beautiful thing it is to enter the stateroom and find a hospital bed and a lift already set up, along with our luggage. Once our baggage goes into the van at home, I don'move it again until we return home. Our hotel room travels with us. In our humble pre-pandemic opinion, cruising was the very best vacation for couples who live with disability.

One challenge with regard to renting equipment when traveling is the cost. Some companies require a minimum rental period of one month. If our need is only for a week, they're happy to deliver the equipment to our hotel and pick it up after a few days or a week, but the charge will be for a full month.

HOTELS

The Americans with Disabilities Act (ADA) applies to hotels, but its implementation varies. Don't count on universal application across the country. Even within one chain, the accessibility between locations and rooms may differ. When we stay in a hotel, I try to record the room number of any rooms that have worked well for us. If we return at a later date, I can give the front desk a heads up. Planning and allowing extra time at check-in, as well as pouring on the grace and patience, will yield a more positive experience. Here are some of our favorite hotel hacks.

- When reserving your room, be sure to clarify your needs. If we will be staying only one night, a roll-in shower is unnecessary. If we are staying for a week, or we are in a hot and humid climate, it is.

- We request the lowest floor possible. This allows us to skip the elevator and makes transporting all the equipment in and out much easier. It also eases concern about exiting in an emergency.
- Call the hotel a day or two ahead to confirm that the room assigned will meet your needs. I always ask whether the bed is Hoyer accessible. Most often, the front desk people don't know what I'm talking about, and it is my turn to educate. I explain that we need a bed frame that is open underneath the entire bed, with a four-inch clearance between the floor and the bed frame. We can't have a room with a fully enclosed box platform.

The typical response is that all their beds have box platforms. I pleasantly persist in asking that either they or someone from housekeeping or maintenance go to the room we will occupy and physically look at the bed. It is amazing how often they call back and say that there is an open frame bed in that room, although no one had ever mentioned this to them. I assure them that this is not surprising and congratulate them on being able to better answer and serve future guests with disabilities.

Despite the best laid plans, we occasionally get a room without an open bed frame. In that case we ask for an upgrade to a suite or room that has a sofa bed or roll-away. These are always lift accessible, although less comfortable. Because we travel with an inflatable, alternating pressure pad mattress, Jerry can handle a less than ideal sofa bed mattress for a few days.

AIRLINES

Not every destination is within driving distance for us. Sometimes we need to fly. In my younger years I loved flying. Now I prefer driving, so we can go at our own pace and haul the equipment we'll need. We're frequently asked how we manage a power wheelchair with airline travel. The process starts when making your reservation. Depending on the length of your flight, you need to choose whether you want a nonstop flight, a direct flight (perhaps including one or more stops but with no plane change), or to change planes. Each person's needs will dictate the best option. When booking, be sure to note that one traveler has a disability and let the airline know what type of help you will need, both at the airport and on the plane.

Most airlines recommend arriving two hours before takeoff. When traveling with someone with a disability, this extra time makes a difference. On some trips we don't need this buffer, but when we do we're glad we factored it in.

We prefer to check our luggage with the curbside skycap, eliminating the need for me to haul it to the ticket counter. When checking luggage with the skycap or at the ticket counter, remind them if you will need an aisle chair and full or partial assistance for boarding. The wheelchair or walker will typically get tagged. This isn't a baggage claim tag but a label that tells the type of batteries in your chair and notes any pre-existing damage. If you are unsure what type of batteries power your chair, contact your manufacturer in advance. Most are dry cells or gel and should present no problem. They'll also ask you the approximate weight of the chair. Tip your skycap generously and head toward your gate.

Medical equipment may be carried onboard at no cost. This is in addition to what your airline deems as free carry-on luggage.

For us, that means a battery charger, a c-pap machine, and all the parts of the wheelchair that come off easily (cushion, head rest, lateral or thigh supports, etc.). I carry an empty canvas bag for easy stowage in the overhead bin of the parts removed. This helps to ensure that we leave with the same parts we came with.

You may think that's a lot of equipment to carry along with a briefcase or purse. I agree. Let me tell you how we learned the hard way to carry those things.

We had scheduled a nonstop flight from Los Angeles to Philadelphia. Before we boarded, the weather in Philadelphia had already shut down arriving flights, and we couldn't get rebooked to Philadelphia for several days. They offered us the choice to spend the four additional nights in Los Angeles (we had already returned our rental van) or travel to Las Vegas. We opted for Las Vegas, thinking that rooms and food would be less expensive there. We also figured that most hotels there would have a wheelchair accessible shuttle to get us to and from the airport, and then we could walk around town.

We exercised good logic—with one flaw. We failed to factor in the lack of a wheelchair battery charger. We had traveled to Los Angeles so often that friends had stored an extra one there for us. Jerry can usually go for a day without charging his chair, but three days would be pushing it, especially traveling through the expanse of airport lands.

We called our friend in LA, who overnighted the battery charger. But this was Friday afternoon, and overnight delivery meant sometime on Monday. Hoping the charger would arrive in time to power his chair for return travel on Tuesday, we sought a secondary backup plan. On Saturday, phone calls connected us to a company in a Las Vegas suburb that had the charger in stock.

Now, how do we get there? This happened before Lyft and Uber. I could take a taxi, but we weren't comfortable with that. Through "a friend of a friend of a friend" connection, we contacted a man who agreed to go to the store Monday morning and pay for the charger (it was a cash-only sale). He drove into the city and came to our hotel. We met him for the first (and only) time and profusely thanked him as we accepted the charger and repaid him for the purchase and his generosity.

Ironically, while in the lobby with this man we received a message that an overnight package had arrived for us at the front desk. For the first three days in Las Vegas, Jerry had not left the room in order to conserve battery power. In fact, he had barely moved around the room. Once his batteries got recharged that last day, he could make it through the airports to arrive finally at home, now carrying two battery chargers.

That is why we always travel with all of the essential equipment. In a travel delay we can wear the same clothes or purchase new ones. But there are some things we can't do without.

Now, back to the airport. Once you check your luggage, head for security. If you can get TSA pre-checked before arrival, do so for each person with you to avoid everyone having to take off shoes or empty carry-ons.

After clearing security, head for your gate and confirm with the gate agent that you will be gate-checking your chair. These agents will put a tag on the chair that alerts personnel at your destination or upon plane change at another airport, so the staff knows to bring your chair to the gate instead of the baggage claim area. They'll also put a luggage claim tag on it.

It will be helpful to let the gate staff know (again) if you will need full or partial assistance to board. From this point on, you wait for boarding. We prefer to sit in the area marked for passengers with disabilities.

About fifteen minutes before general boarding, a gate agent will check in with you and let you know the plan. At the proper time they, and those assisting with the transfer, along with one person in your party, will board. This is where the real fun begins.

At the end of the jetway where it joins the plane's door, you have the option to walk on if able or transfer to an aisle chair. An aisle chair is a skinny chair on wheels designed to move through the beyond-narrow aisle of a plane.

Some crews who assist with this transfer are skilled, and the movement proceeds like clockwork. More often, you must direct the process, being sure that those who are assisting listen to you and help in the ways most beneficial *for you*. Jerry says, "There is a reason people with disabilities are the first ones on and the last ones off the plane. It's ugly, and the airlines don't want anyone else to see. In fact, I don't want to be seen then, either."

In the scores of flights we've taken, we've had an uncomfortable experience only once, but now I'm always prepared. After we had settled into our seats, the lead flight attendant asked me whether, in the event of an emergency, I could get Jerry off the plane on my own. I answered, "I'm not sure. I might need help." The attendant replied that we might have to deplane if we would need help in an emergency.

I asked her to ask me the question again. She did, and this time I replied, "Yes. He's my husband, the one I love. I'll do whatever it takes to get him off the plane in an emergency." Neither of us said anything more, and we made it to our destination. Honestly, could she have told me that anyone else on that plane would have known how they would react in the event of a genuine emergency?

Once we're on the plane, the wheelchair gets moved to the tarmac and loaded into the baggage hold. When we land, we wait for all of the other passengers to leave. Often, we may still wait after that while they bring the wheelchair to the gate. The transfer off the plane is the reverse of the boarding process.

RENTAL CARS

If we need to rent accessible transportation, we arrange for it weeks in advance. Public and hotel transportation are becoming more accessible, especially in major cities. Even though the hotel may own an appropriate vehicle, however, that doesn't mean it will be in service or that they will have a designated driver who knows how to operate it. Planning ahead adds time to our preparation but saves time and stress upon arrival.

Several companies rent wheelchair-accessible minivans, but all require prior arrangements and aren't as cost effective as a typical rental car. A wheelchair accessible rental van will cost three to five times the rate pf a rental car. Most companies will meet us with a driver at the baggage curb to sign over the vehicle and explain the drop-off plan. We know to be prepared, because accessible vehicles may not come with handicapped license plates or a hang tag. So, we've learned to pack our own hang tag and retrieve it when we return the vehicle.

TRAINS

Jerry and I have taken only one train trip. The Amtrak Auto Train travels from Lorton, Virginia, to Sanford, Florida. Our experience was pleasant, and we recommend it to others. Earlier ticket purchase means a lower price, so we booked early and paid for travel insurance in case we needed to make a change. Taking a vehicle on the auto train requires two purchases. One is the passenger ticket, whether in a private berth or coach seats, and the other is for the vehicle.

We chose coach seating, which provided a spacious area for Jerry and his wheelchair. My seat faced him, and we had a great deal of room for baggage, although we left most of our luggage in the locked van for the trip. On board, we carried light snacks; a card game or two; some pillows and blankets; and our computers, iPads, and phones. Our assigned seats were in a car next to the lobby of restrooms. It was easy to move between areas.

They sold food from a cafe in an upper car. I easily went upstairs and brought the food back. If you want high quality food, we understand that this requires a private berth if you're unable to access the dining car.

The best part for us was the sixteen to eighteen hours during which we didn't have to pay attention to traffic. We napped, played games, wrote, and read. Our train trip concluded a nearly four-week road trip of 3600 miles and meeting with 190 people. We were exhausted, and the train allowed us to decompress and realign our minds before arriving home.

WHEN TRAVEL STOPS

Conversations about the pace at which we can continue to travel have been frequent in recent months. We're still talking through what we gain from the journeys versus what the travel takes out of us now that we're nearing retirement. We keep our eyes open for someone who may want to join us as a traveling companion and share the driving, loading, and unloading. An arrangement like this would allow us to travel longer into our senior years.

EMBRACING TRAVEL/ADVENTURE

1. Do you and your spouse travel together? If not, is there some place you'd personally like to explore?
2. If you do travel together but sense that a change is coming, set a date to talk together about the situation and decide how to proceed.
3. Research in advance as best you can. Then commit to being flexible and enjoying the journey as much as the destination.

EMBRACING YOUR FRIENDS

1. If your friends seem interested in travel, gently encourage them.
2. Perhaps you might offer to travel with them, at least for one trip, to offer support and help as they learn.
3. When you travel for business or pleasure, try to make note of accessibility concerns and share viable opportunities with your friends.

PSALM 139:9-10

"If I rise on the wings of the dawn, if I settle on the far side of the sea, even there your hand will guide me, your right hand will hold me fast."

PRAYER

Heavenly Father, thank you for the amazing world you created and the discoveries you gave to many people to allow us to travel in multiple ways to nearly any destination in the world. Give us the courage to be adventurous and explore, as well as the peace and contentment to know when it's time to stay home. Amen.

ELEVEN

MAKE ROOM FOR FUN

By this point, I hope you have seen that humor is important to Jerry and me. In fact, if you were to ask him for his favorite story about me, he would likely reply, "Her second-grade report card." My teacher had added this comment: "Joan would be a much better student if she did not laugh at the misfortunes of others."

Not my proudest moment, but an ironic foreshadowing of my future. Today, I still love to laugh, but rather than laughing *at* others I now laugh as a tool to get through difficult times. It's all about the adage "Better to laugh than cry." Though I still do plenty of that, too.

I hope you and your spouse laugh often and loudly together. It's a wonderful way to develop a stronger relationship. Employing humor every day keeps the harsh realities of disability from ruling our lives.

Sometimes daily life is challenging:

. . . we have to wait over six weeks for a wheelchair repair that is covered under warranty. . . . our morning attendant called out sick.

. . . our spouse's body worked on its own schedule, and a restroom break is necessary *now*.

. . . someone forgot to check accessibility for an event, and now we can't attend.

These situations at the time are rarely humorous. Nor are they intentional disruptions by our spouse. Facing them with a "this is life" attitude will relieve a lot of tension along the way and maybe even reveal a funny moment.

THE PERKS OF DISABILITY

Early in our marriage, we watched late night television and enjoyed many of David Letterman's Top Ten lists. This led me to create our own Top Ten List of reasons to marry a man who uses a wheelchair. For now, will you prepare a drum roll as I share our list?

10. You don't have to stand on tiptoes to style his hair.
9. You get great parking spots.
8. You have lots of fun gadgets to "play with" and exercise creativity with as you learn to repair them.
7. Sometimes you get to fly first-class for the price of coach.
6. Shopping is easier when you hang the bags on his chair.
5. The back of his clothes doesn't need repair or ironing.
4. He provides free strength training and aerobic exercise.
3. There are lots of places at home to hide his gifts where he can't find them.
2. The toilet seat is always down.
1. God created him in his own image to be my wonderful protector, encourager, comforter, lover, and friend.

DATING

Date night is a concept that is easier to talk about than maintain. Many people I speak with feel stuck. They wonder after so many years, or kids, or illnesses, whether dates matter.

Yes.

Dating matters.

God designed marriage as the foundational relationship for families. Strong dates build healthy families, which establish healthy communities. Dating keeps our relationship fresh and fun, reignites early passion and commitment, and reminds us of why we fell in love.

But the desire for a date night doesn't eliminate schedule challenges. Work, kids' activities, medical appointments, and therapies demand time. So should our marriages. Over the course of our marriage, Jerry and I have tried several approaches. Our experiences may help you brainstorm ideas.

During our first couple of years, we designated every Friday night, or the second and fourth Friday or Saturday, as date night. We found this plan difficult to remember and experienced challenges with getting into a rhythm.

Then we came up with this idea. Because we had married on the eleventh of November, we set aside the eleventh of every month for a date. We have instant variety because the eleventh falls on a different day of the week each month. If our plans will require most of a day, we look forward to a Saturday. On Tuesdays we may take advantage of the discount at the movie theater. Thursday dates may include an evening stroll around the outdoor mall where musicians perform each week.

Jerry plans for the odd months, and I arrange for the even months. We seek to choose an activity our mate would enjoy, even if it might not necessarily be our own preference. If we're unsure, we ask for our spouse's input. I keep a list of ideas we've discussed, so that, when it's my turn, I have several options to consider. These include baseball functions, restaurants he prefers, movies he has mentioned, and things he has offhandedly stated that he'd like to try.

The eleventh has become a sacred day in our calendars, and we let nothing interfere unless we both agree to reschedule.

Setting apart the day of the month on which we married reminds us of our commitment to one another. We honor our promise with our "month-a-versary" and have even established a contest around who can say "Happy Month-A-Versary" to the other earlier on the eleventh. The winner kindly gloats, while the other expresses remorse and vows to win the next time.

We've each stayed awake until midnight or set an alarm for 12:01 a.m. in order to be the first to text the other. I've written it with lipstick on the bathroom mirror, noting the time, so that when Jerry gets up he sees that I remembered first. Silly? Sappy? Yes. But our game reminds us that we're in this together and that our shared life is fun.

For the first five years we read aloud our marriage vows on our dates. This practice was a great way to check ourselves against what we had said we would do and determine in which areas we needed to pay closer attention. Saying and hearing those words reinforced them in our hearts and minds. Although we no longer recite them monthly, we often do on our anniversary.

Sometimes we stay home and watch a movie. At other times we go out to dinner with another couple. We may watch the video of our wedding, go for a walk, play a table game, dream about a vacation we want to take, or ponder how we want our retirement years to look. We don't talk about work or finances or bring up any serious issues. Phones get silenced and put away. We focus on one another.

If you or your partner travels for work, and one of you is away for date night, you might choose a movie you will both enjoy and start it at the same time. Keep a phone call live while you are mutually viewing. You can order the same food and eat together by video chat. This bridges the gap in the case of physical absence.

Over the years we added a second, more flexible, monthly date, always on the same day of the month. Sometimes we talk through a situation or concern, as long as we both agree in advance to do so. Even then, we try to add something fun and engaging. Or we read a book together and discuss it or share in Bible study.

My best encouragement to you: don't get hung up over how often you date, when you date, or what you do. Make dating frequent and meaningful. Find something that works for you and your family. Try it for a few months, and then adapt as needed.

Melissa related that, when her daughters started preschool, she and her husband found that evening dates weren't realistic, so they committed to a weekly lunch date on Thursdays. They continue this practice now that their girls are adults.

For some, the budget can't accommodate a babysitter, caregiver, or respite worker. It won't improve your relationship if you go into debt for a date. One solution is to put younger kids to bed earlier one night a week to create alone time. Order dinner in.

As the kids get older, offer a special treat like a movie night or other activity in which they can engage only when Mom and Dad have a date. Your teens might think they have won, but you know that the real prize is your quiet evening over a special dinner or while sharing a long, leisurely cup of coffee and dessert.

Extended family members may host the kids one night a week or month. Who doesn't like to go to their aunt's or grandma's and get spoiled? Try not to use that time—at least not in its entirety—to do household projects or grocery shop. Set aside time for your beloved.

I love hearing of a couple who play *their song* each morning and dance together before he heads out to work. What a lovely way to start the day.

Years passed before we added a second date day to our calendar, so begin with a plan that will build success. Dates strengthen the connection between you and your husband or wife. Through dating you remind one another, even when you may not get as much alone time as you'd like, that you still have each other's hearts. There is no one in the world you would rather be with. It doesn't matter how long you have been married or the state of your relationship.

Start today.

And have fun and celebrate another one of God's amazing creations—the two of you.

OUR FIRST THANKSGIVING

We were married in November, so the holiday season was well under way when we got back from our honeymoon. I was excited to cook our first Thanksgiving meal and share it with my husband.

The alarm went off early for me to get up to make the stuffing and prep the turkey for roasting. I made everything I could from scratch. It was a long day, but it was truly a labor of love. I set the table with our newly gifted china. When everything was ready, I called Jerry to the table.

We sat at the table laden with food, holding hands as Jerry offered our thanks back to God. He had barely completed the "amen" when tears streaked my face.

"Sweetheart, what's wrong?"

"I don't feel good," I cried.

Jerry asked me why I had said nothing earlier and had gone to all the effort of the meal preparation that could have waited until I felt well.

"Because I wanted to make you our first Thanksgiving." And with that, I was done. I went to bed and curled up under the blankets while Jerry ate our first Thanksgiving meal alone.

I was too sick to get up and clear the table or refrigerate the remaining food. Jerry called a friend, who came and stashed away leftovers and washed all the dishes.

At the time, this was not a funny story. Today it is one we reminisce about most every Thanksgiving.

HOLIDAYS, BIRTHDAYS, AND ANNIVERSARIES

God incorporated celebrations as a normal part of life. And he is quite the partier. If you have any doubt, read about the Israelite festivals in the Old Testament (Leviticus 23) and how long he instructed each of them to be celebrated. You may not take a month off from work and other duties to celebrate a milestone, but you can do something.

Develop traditions unique to the two of you. It's okay if you celebrate in ways that others may think odd. Do you serve the same meal for every birthday? Do you fill the house with balloons? Is there a favorite movie you repeatedly watch or a podcast you listen to? Perhaps a sporting event that requires a little extra savings to enjoy once a year? Instead of a cake, perhaps you have pudding or something savory instead of sweet.

Look for reasons beyond the obvious birthdays and wedding anniversary to celebrate. An extensive project at work got finished? Party. It has been ten years since your diagnosis of disability—celebrate that God continues to sustain you. Technological advancements have developed sufficiently to give voice to a spouse who lost theirs? Rejoice. The durable medical equipment company finally returned your call? Kick up your heels—or kick the tires.

Do you get the idea? Celebration doesn't have to be elaborate. Decorations are unnecessary, though having the guest of honor wear a silly hat may add to the joy (and embarrassment). Such frivolity does not require tons of planning or time. Acknowledging in a way that is meaningful to both of you works.

Christmas festivities were underway. This was the first Christmas Jerry wouldn't be with his family. I wanted to bring a taste of home to his West coast Christmas and do something special for him. I'd heard Jerry and his family speak of buckeyes, the candy that looks like the nut of Ohio's buckeye tree. These were one of his favorite treats, though I'd never tried one.

While he was out, I called his brother to ask how to make buckeyes. Eric directed me to call Aunt Dollene, whom I'd met only once. Of course, she welcomed my call and gave me the recipe and explained how they should look when finished. I didn't have all the exact ingredients she mentioned but figured that what I had could substitute sufficiently. Boy, was I wrong.

When Jerry came home, sheets of parchment oozing with peanut butter and chocolate puddles surrounded me. "I tried to make buckeyes." Somehow, he contained his laughter and used a spoon to indulge in some "California buckeyes," telling me how good they tasted. They weren't what he was used to, but he was grateful I'd made the effort. As the years went on, I learned to use the correct ingredients, and my buckeyes came out as expected. Making buckeyes has become one of our family traditions.

WHEN THINGS DON'T GO AS PLANNED—STILL CELEBRATE

We had often talked and shared elaborate dreams about our twenty-fifth anniversary. As the day drew closer, my thought changed to, *As long as we can be together to celebrate our silver anniversary on the eleventh of November, I'll be okay.*

This hope quashed the remorse I had experienced when COVID-19 prevented me from celebrating my birthday with my husband. With a three-week gap between my birthday and our anniversary, I felt optimistic. I should have been a bit more specific about my wish.

The day before our anniversary dawned, Jerry and I were both feeling well and looking forward to celebrating this milestone together. Our plans included visiting several jewelers to price the repair and enhancement of my engagement ring. Later we would travel to a nearby town for dinner and visit a new restaurant neighbors raved about.

On our anniversary eve, Jerry left the house in the late morning, saying he had some errands to do. I knew this was code for "I am going to get you a card and flowers." I didn't note what time he left, but as the afternoon wore on I wondered what was taking so long.

I was relieved to see his van in our driveway when I returned from a trip to the bank. As I entered through the garage, he greeted me with the words, "I had a little accident today."

A quick glance at my hubby didn't show any signs of an accident. My mind flashed back to the van. It looked okay. I asked, "With another vehicle?"

"No, just my wheelchair."

"What happened?"

"I went to get you roses and chocolate." This sounded like a good start.

"I parked at the far end of the lot. When I left the store, I rolled down the sidewalk to the curb cut. I saw the crosshatches on the pavement. Usually, they're painted only as wide as the ramp. But not these. I didn't notice that the lines were three feet wider than the sidewalk cut and rolled off the curb and fell forward in my chair."

I cringed.

"My body pitched forward as the two front tires settled on the blacktop while the two back tires stayed on the sidewalk."

"Please tell me you were wearing your seatbelt?" I begged. He was, which had prevented him from doing a face-plant on the blacktop. But there was more.

"When my front tires hit the pavement, my footrests folded up toward my knees."

He didn't have to say more. I pictured his upper body pitching downward while his ankles pushed upward.

"I yelled for help, and people seemed to come out of nowhere. They asked what they should do. 'First, push my upper body back in the chair so I can sit up. Next, I need to get my wheelchair on one level. Can you help lift me off the sidewalk onto the pavement?'

"Once I was stable, several of the people suggested they call 911, but, other than my adrenalin pumping, I couldn't sense any injuries. I assured them that I would get into my van and calm down before driving home."

The story ended. Jerry handed me the roses and apologized that one bud had broken off the stem in the mishap.

I questioned my tough guy about potential injuries and the need for medical treatment. His ankles were sore, and he suspected he had sprained them. He suggested that we elevate his legs and apply ice. Jerry assured me that he did not need to go to urgent care. When I took his shoes off, there were no obvious broken bones, bruising, or swelling. His plan seemed appropriate.

My loving husband tried to convince me that this situation would not thwart our plans for the following day. I reminded him that plans could change and that my top priority was his well-being. We had set our starting positions for the negotiations to come.

Waking up on November 11, 2020, we faced a day much different from the one we had celebrated twenty-five years earlier. Gorgeous colors and the warm California sun had provided the backdrop to our wedding day. Now a hurricane and tornado watch targeted our home in Florida. At the very least, we were in for torrential rains. This was not a day to get in and out of the van to visit jewelers.

On our wedding day his feet had sported mismatched socks, while on this day his bare feet and ankles swelled, showing off a rainbow of colors.

We snuggled up at home, as much as possible, and watched "our movie," *Sleepless in Seattle*.

Jerry, wanting to redeem the day for me, insisted that we brave the weather to go out to dinner. He could still drive without pain since he uses hand controls instead of foot pedals. His feet pointed at odd angles as he entered the van, and he struggled to get properly positioned behind the steering wheel. He gasped when his ankles took another hit in his effort to make the tight turn.

Anguished to see him in pain, I used my best mama bear tone to state authoritatively, "That's it. We're not going out. Let's go back in the house."

Jerry did not argue.

After we had dried off and regrouped emotionally, we agreed that being together is what our anniversary is all about. It's not about what we do, where we go, or how much money we spend. It's acknowledging the excellent gift God gave us in one another. We celebrated with food I brought home from a nearby restaurant.

Traditionally, the milestone of twenty-five years of marriage is called the Silver Anniversary. But we're not ones to follow ritual. We're calling ours the Ice Anniversary.

For those interested in the end of the story, one week later, he agreed to go to the emergency room. It was then we learned he'd broken both ankles.

EMBRACING CELEBRATIONS

1. Remember together dates you've shared in the past. Reminisce about some of your favorites and recall what made them special. When was the last time you had a date without kids? Make a plan for one in the next ten days.
2. Do you have a celebration tradition unique to your family? Can you start one?
3. Our dreams and expectations can change in a moment. How can you begin today to celebrate in little and big ways?

EMBRACING YOUR FRIENDS

1. Offer to babysit the kids, giving your friends time together for a date. If there are no kids, ask how you can help the spouse with disability prepare for a special date.
2. Deliver a meal or dessert or invite your friends, and maybe others, over to celebrate a birthday, anniversary, or other special occasion.
3. Suggest and schedule a double date with your friends.

1 TIMOTHY 6:17 NLT

"Their trust should be in God, who richly gives us all we need for our enjoyment."

PRAYER

God, sometimes the busyness of life and the demands of disability leave little time for us. Show us how we can make time for one another. Teach us to laugh together and to celebrate your wonderful gift of us. Amen.

TWELVE

AGING AND DISABILITY

Life can be a paradox. Throughout their childhood and adult years, people living with disability may strive to appear normal or compare themselves to those deemed typical. Yet as the population ages, many formerly average people join the world of disability. Wheelchairs, walkers, canes, large print, or amplified hearing devices are no longer unusual factors.

Until recently, there were few senior adult role models with disabilities; medical science didn't expect anyone to live that long. Some in the medical profession still hold that belief, it seems. But we *are* living longer. Jerry, and others around our age, are on the cusp of setting the stage for what it is like to grow old with a disability.

REFLECTIONS AT SIXTY

On his sixtieth birthday, Jerry shared the following reflections:

> "Not that long ago, I thought of sixty as older. I now see it as middle aged. After all, my grandfather lived to be 102.
>
> "I haven't found a playbook for disability at sixty. When I was growing up, there weren't any examples, or at least ones I noticed. Most families affected by disability were just trying to make it through the school year, the month, or that day.
>
> "One thing I'm sure about at sixty is that there are things I wish I had known when I was younger. I'm grateful to be learning them now instead of in ten years. For example, life isn't as hard when I stop expecting it to be easy. I understood that life with disability could be difficult, but I never really thought about the fact that people without disabilities also face challenges. Many of the obstacles I face are common to men. Some of my challenges are similar to those faced by other men who have been married for twenty-plus years, entrepreneurs who start new ventures in retirement, and leaders. If there is a difference, it's this: disability and its effects are ubiquitous. They color every other area of my life.
>
> "I wish I had been more focused in my twenties and thirties. Sometimes it feels like I squandered those years. I wish I had some of that energy back, though my mind still thinks I do. That eighty percent of people in their sixties and seventies would agree is exactly my point.

"The difference is, when you are a person with a disability, living takes a larger village. Nobody makes it through life alone. However, we all know people for whom it looks from the outside as though they do. Nobody accomplishes anything worthwhile alone.

"This flies against the disability mantra of independence: I've got to do this myself. A close cousin is another disability maxim: I have to be twice as good just to be noticed. Unfortunately, this self-defeating assumption is part of every minority group's thinking. If we are doing what God has built us to do, being twice as good as someone else is not the point. That's harder to believe and actualize than it is to say.

"There are some advantages to sixty. I survived a lot of things my parents probably didn't think I would. Many of my biggest worries never materialized. It's okay to be wrong or fail. Just make sure you learn from it.

"I pray I have another twenty or thirty years. I don't know if I will. There are some things that are easier because of the commonness of aging, but not everything. For example, travel, losing weight because of my lack of mobility, and the time required to do everything is more difficult now than it used to be. My mind thinks I still can, but my body says I can't. I need more sleep. I need more recovery time after a season of significant activity, like a week of camp, a conference, or speaking engagements. Relationships matter more. I also find that typical men over the age of fifty-five or sixty identify with me more now than they did years ago."

THE AGING CAREGIVING SPOUSE

Aging, of course, also affects the caregiver and the marriage relationship. Grace has been a caregiving spouse longer than I have. I appreciate her example and wisdom:

> "From the caregiving spouse perspective, things change, too. My stamina is definitely not what it used to be. His body is aging, and this brings new challenges, which inevitably surprise us because we've been dealing with disability for over thirty-five years together. Sometimes we say to each other, 'This is a fresh problem we haven't encountered yet.' You'd think we'd have seen it all by now. But that's not the case. And then we start anew to track the problem and try to find a solution.
>
> "We talk about aging often. It's the only way to work through it. As we get older, it is difficult to just do things spontaneously without so much planning. When life gets really tough, we play the Blessing Game, a back-and-forth time of naming our blessings. One of us will begin with 'sunshine.' The other will reply, 'church family,' and so on to get our minds off the problem at hand."

When I asked another friend, Linda, about the impact of her husband's disability on their marriage, she didn't think she had anything to contribute. After thinking about it, though, she shared:

> "God has been extraordinarily kind and merciful to shield my thoughts and keep me focused on my purpose in our marriage relationship. It has not been an easy journey. No marriage journey is easy . . . being

affected by a disability certainly adds to the stress for both of us. Life has always been full. We have raised three children, homeschooled, raised other people's kids, been active in church life. But the older we get, and the closer we get to retiring, the more I realize just how incredibly difficult our marriage has been. I can only say that it's a God thing. Glen and I have a deep love OF God and love FOR each other. And we've stood up against the pressures of life only because God has willed it and us. The older I get, the more pain I live with. The older Glen gets, the more I realize how very difficult everything—I mean EVERYTHING—is for him. NOTHING is easy. This makes me more grateful for God's kindness and goodness to us both."

I (Joan) have noticed that, as we get older, we've become wiser in realizing that our time, health, and energy are worth at least as much as, or perhaps more than, our dollars. Money isn't the sole, or even the primary, factor in decision making. We have a mental grid through which we weigh decisions. This matrix includes questions like:

- What will this require of our time? If we say yes to this, to what will we say no?
- Do we need to plan a sleep-in day or a day off in the middle of travel or during a busy week?
- Serving and taking part in the same event may not mean that we are spending time together. For activities that span several days, do we need to build in time to reconnect?
- What will be happening in the weeks before and after? To what have we already committed?

It is critical to remember that even life-giving opportunities will incur a cost to our time and energy. It's not fun saying no to a visit with friends or turning down an activity we know we'd enjoy. Sometimes it feels downright wimpy to say no when other friends are saying yes. But their life is not like ours, and ours is not like theirs.

Three times over the last year I've had to acknowledge that the reality of aging as a caregiver is hitting me hard. One time it was because of an injured knee while traveling nine-hundred miles from home. Another involved multiple weeks of low back spasms. The third was a neck injury. Each one of these situations affected both Jerry's lifestyle and mine, including the level of care I could give to him.

While healing, we talked often and arrived at several decisions.

When traveling, I will not be the one to load and unload the van at every stop. We'll either travel with a third party or request help from someone at our destination.

I have to alter my day-to-day activities. My back and neck are degenerating. That is not unusual for women of my age. I can no longer pick up two babies at once in the church nursery, haul eight grocery bags in a single trip, or run from dawn to past dusk.

My new reality is this: my husband needs my knees, back, and neck. I need to evaluate every opportunity presented to me, considering its effect on my ability to stay strong for him as long as I can.

Jerry has also made a decision. It's time to refresh his application for attendant services through our state. He'll still be on a waiting list, but life circumstances may move us higher up the priority list.

While it was hard to make some of these choices, a peace has settled over us. There are many routes one can take through life. Knowing that we've crossed another bridge together on our journey of aging with disability brings comfort and rest.

WHEN WORDS FADE

If your spouse can no longer speak to you with words, do their eyes or their smile convey thanks to you? Is the only time they seem calm and comforted when they are with you? Does their anxiety level lessen when you are in their line of vision? These are glimmers of their appreciation. Don't overlook these gems.

Robertson McQuilkin was president of Columbia Bible College when I attended. I had the privilege of getting to know him and his wife, Muriel, when we worshiped at the same church. Many years later, Alzheimer's raged through Muriel. In 1990 Robertson stepped down from his role of president to care for his beloved. In *Living by Vows*, he shared this story:[19]

"The board arranged for a companion to stay in our home so I could go daily to the office. During those two years, it became increasingly difficult to keep Muriel home. As soon as I left, she would take out after me. With me she was content; without me she was distressed, sometimes terror stricken. The walk to school is a mile round trip. She would make that trip as many as ten times a day. Sometimes at night, when I helped her undress, I found bloody feet. When I told our family doctor, he choked up.

"'Such love,' he said simply. Then, after a moment, 'I have a theory that the characteristics developed across the years come out at times like these.' I wish I loved God like that—desperate to be near him at all times. Thus, she teaches me, day by day."

LOOKING AHEAD

Robert Browning wrote, "Grow old along with me! The best is yet to be."[20]

I asked both Grace and Jerry a few more questions, beginning with "*What are the things you look forward to as you grow older with your spouse?*"

Grace: "Being together. We really do like each other. Through the Covid quarantine, we discovered this. We began a game tournament between the two of us. And we started delivering flowers on the weekends to people from our church. It's a way to encourage others through the isolation."

Jerry: "Time. Spending more time with you. Five years ago, I would have said travel, but we're traveling less now. The older I get, I'm always a day closer to seeing Jesus. We both are. I enjoy looking forward to that together."

"*Are there ways in which you think disability has better prepared you for aging?*"

Grace: "Disability has hopefully made me more patient, more caring, more tuned in to the needs of others, more interested in building relationships."

Jerry: "I know how to advocate for me and my family. I know where to call, and I know not to give up. I don't always get it right, but it has taught me what is important."

"What strategies are you using to assist with the challenges of aging, disability, and caregiving?"

Grace: "Philip is teaching me how to do the accounting of our money because he's the one who keeps track of this. Also, he urges me to get away and visit out-of-town family whenever I feel I need a break from being his full-time caregiver. I really appreciate that. It helps me redirect my focus, and it helps him to appreciate more the way I care for him.

"We also like to get together with friends who are in a similar situation with a disability. It helps to bounce ideas off one another."

Jerry: "Denial, though it's not a strategy I'd recommend. I'm trying to grow my earning power. I've got fewer years now to put away for retirement. I want to maximize my earning potential."

A BEAUTIFUL, BROKEN BODY

Bill Gaither shared a story that touched my heart. I am sure it will yours, too. He related the story of his friends, Ann and Nathan Smith, who had been married for multiple decades. Nathan's body was now bent over from living with a disability. One morning he expressed sorrow to his beloved wife, Ann, that she had to see his bent and broken body. Ann responded, "Nathan, I've seen Jesus live through your body for more than sixty years, and it is beautiful."

EMBRACING AGING

1. Melanie Wilber wrote in *Home for Christmas*, "Their marriage was a blanket of grace that had been so many years in the making." Is your marriage a blanket of grace? If so, how? If not, how can you change that, beginning today?
2. Have you played the blessing game? If not, follow Philip and Grace's lead and start a round with your loved one.
3. Can you talk about your fears of aging and handling life with your spouse? Sharing the burden and fear lessens their grip.

EMBRACING YOUR FRIENDS

1. Listen when your friends want to talk about their thoughts on aging. Identify wherever you can. Let them share without judgment.
2. Ask your friends for advice as you face your own senior years. They may have already encountered a similar situation and would love to help you.
3. If you notice areas in which your friends need help as they age, work with them to find resources in your community or local church.

ISAIAH 46:4

"Even to your old age and gray hairs I am he, I am he who will sustain you. I have made you and I will carry you; I will sustain you and I will rescue you."

PRAYER

Father God, the old hymn says, "O God, our help in ages past, our hope for years to come . . ." We echo those words. Thank you for being our sustainer through every day and every year. Our times are in your hands. We thank you for each day you give us life and breath together. May we honor you with our moments. Thank you for the gift of growing older together. Amen.

SECTION THREE

LIFE IN COMMUNITY

THIRTEEN

HARD TRUTHS

We who live with disability in our family, whether of our spouse or another family member, attend to their physical, emotional, and spiritual needs. But we can't do it alone. The previous chapters addressed couples living with disability. This one speaks primarily to those in our churches and communities who want to better understand our lives. I'll cover some challenges of life with disability, as well as a few of the resulting misconceptions outsiders often express.

DISABILITY TAKES A VILLAGE

Several times Jerry and I have been told we make living with disability look easy. *Really? How do we do that?* "Easy" is not a word either of us would use to describe our life. But it's not as hard as some think because we've developed routines and practices. Unless something out of the ordinary arises, we hum along at our normal pace.

Late last year the *Tampa Evening News* reported on a woman and her adult daughter who were charged with neglect and sentenced to prison. The person they neglected and watched die was their husband and father, a quadriplegic.

Once is too often. But, sadly, this is not an isolated incident.

Several years ago, a Philadelphia mother left her twenty-one-year-old son with cerebral palsy alone by a creek for over a week. As he lay there, with only a blanket and a Bible, she visited her boyfriend.

The son, after having been found alive by a passerby, received treatment at a hospital before being moved into the care of his extended family. The authorities located the mother and arrested her.

This story enrages listeners. People unfamiliar with the family berate the mother, call her names, and ask, "*How could she?*"

This *is* horrendous. I don't condone the actions of these women. It *was* wrong to endanger their family member's life. I do not excuse these caregivers, yet I have compassion for all three women because I have some understanding of what they may have felt.

Caregiving is hard.

Many of you reading this are nodding in agreement. Even though the one I care for is verbal and can assist with his needs, caregiving can be exhausting.

It is relentless.

It is lonely.

There is no end in sight.

Some say these family caregivers should have sought services to help—as though it were that easy. Securing services can be a full-time job even without the caregiving part. Even if funding is available, the wait can be exceptionally long—even years. Professional caregivers are among the lowest paid class of workers. This makes finding an appropriate and well-trained caregiver difficult. Raising awareness of this reality can lead to genuine change in supporting caregivers.

Yet even positive changes in terms of funding, services, and waiting lists would not be enough.

The answer to the challenges of life with disability and caregiving goes beyond money or better services. The answer is Jesus Christ. He is the only hope that is greater—infinitely greater—than anything this world offers. His hope carries into eternity and has no waiting list.

How will caregivers, and those they love, learn about this hope? We rarely see them streaming through the doors of our local churches, and yet Christians are called to care for each other. This includes loving one another and bearing one another's burdens (John 16:34, Galatians 6:2).

Might these stories have ended differently if Christians in the community had been there to encourage, help with care, and let these caregivers know there is a better way than neglect or abandonment?

We'll never know.

These tragic accounts call us to action. It's time to build the passion, capacity, and burden within the Christian community to come alongside families affected by disability.

TAKING THE FIRST STEP—FAMILIES

Families affected by disability often perceive typical families as having more time, energy, or resources than they do. Some no doubt do, but it is more likely that our perceptions are skewed. Instead, ask yourselves, "How are we building into our community?"

It's unfair to expect everyone else to see us and help with our needs if we don't attempt to see them, too. We might start with a text to ask how *they* are doing. Or a quick email or social media post following up on something in *their* lives.

Sometimes our community doesn't know what to do. We may appear strong and invincible. Or our needs may seem so overwhelming that they feel unequipped to help.

Building a relationship will open understanding. We need to embrace others before we expect them to embrace us.

TAKING THE FIRST STEP—COMMUNITIES

For the community not affected by disability, the biggest challenge of disability is that it is *so daily*. My husband says he could handle life with a disability better if he could set it aside for a long weekend or a brief vacation. But life doesn't work that way.

The dailiness of disability is wearing. Affected families can't always articulate their needs. Some days we aren't particularly grace-filled when expressing them. At other times the repetitive necessary details are just too much. Please don't let us turn you away. We need you. If our name comes to mind, pray for us, drop off a plate of cookies or a cup of coffee, send a "thinking-of-you" text, or call before you head to the grocery store to see if we need anything.

If you do not know anyone with a disability, ask God to open your eyes to someone in your community. As you drive around your town, look for homes that have a ramp up to the door or a marked accessible parking spot. Notice the bagger at your grocery store who may have special needs.

THE COST OF DISABILITY

Disability is expensive. Whether it's mobility equipment, hearing aids, a modified vehicle, a specific therapy, or something else, insurance rarely covers it. And if it does, the co-pay may be prohibitive. When I'm asked why this is the case, I often respond, "Because we're a captive audience."

If you're part of a family affected by disability, this isn't news. However, this is likely new information if you don't know anyone with a disability or have only casual acquaintances. If that's you, perhaps you think that insurance or government-based programs and services cover all the costs. If only that were true . . .

Scores, maybe hundreds of articles, exist about the impact of financial tension on marriage. Add to this what author Amy Kenney describes in *My Body Is Not a Prayer Request*: "Crip tax is a term for the way society charges disabled people for being disabled. The costs of mobility devices, medical care, and assistive technology are weighty. One study found that disabled adults in the United States pay an extra $10,000–$30,000 just for being disabled—per year. Every year."

If you've wondered why your friends with disabilities, even if they seem to have decent jobs, never have money for a meal out or a trip to the movies, let me explain. It may have nothing to do with how they manage their finances and everything to do with the prohibitive costs of disability that require every dollar available.

Consider this breakdown of some numbers:

If we have insurance to help cover our needs or get help from a state vocational rehabilitation department, we are typically responsible for paying twenty to eighty percent of the total bill. To give you an idea of what that means, consider the following: a basic manual wheelchair averages $1,200–$1,500. A power wheelchair fitted to an individual's specific needs runs $20,000–$40,000 and sometimes more. Replacement batteries are about $800.

The price for a simple ramp for a home with only one step is $500–$3,000.

Modifying a narrow doorway costs about $700–$2,500.

Attendant care rates average $10–50 per hour, depending on what part of the country you live in. They often require a minimum two- or four-hour shift, even if only one hour of care is needed.

To convert a minivan to accessibility for a driver in a wheelchair will require upward of $30,000–$60,000. This is on top of the purchase price of the vehicle. The total is less if the person with a disability is only a passenger.

Families will spend around $9,000 for an average bathroom conversion.

These costs are over and above the purchase of a basic vehicle or home. I don't present these numbers to sound sensational or ask for your pity or financial contributions. I share them to educate you, our friends.

GET A JOB

Everyone needs meaningful work. Rarely does a person with a disability secure a job fitting their level of knowledge and talent with a livable wage that is on par with that of their nondisabled coworkers. In one city where we lived, we had a friend who had multiple postgraduate degrees and was an inventor. The only job he could get with his difficult-to-understand speech and spastic movements was to round up carts at the grocery store.

Jerry most often created his own job, always in the nonprofit sector. One day his brother asked, "Have you considered a job working with people who could pay you?" Thankfully, the joy and blessing we receive working with people affected by disabilities enhance the paycheck. His brother knew that.

Reliable transportation to a job may be a deterrent. Paratransit services are better than they used to be but still have much room for improvement in terms of reliability. Private accessible transport companies are increasing in number but are often unaffordable. They have a pickup fee, typically $30–45 for each time you load into their vehicle, and then a per mile charge of one to three dollars. When our van broke down at a medical appointment, we had no choice but to hire a private service to drive Jerry the nine miles home. The bill was $248.

Many who live with a disability find that their bodies don't always follow a nine-to-five schedule. A pastor who incurred a disability from an auto accident commented that disability is itself a part-time job. Employers may be hesitant to hire someone with a disability because of the accommodation that may be needed.

The most maddening barrier Jerry and I faced while working together was when a manager asked him, "Do you really do the work, or does Joan do it and you're just the public face?"

The idea of having a community, whether family, friends, neighbors, or church members, is foreign to many families with disabilities. This is heartbreaking. But it doesn't have to be fatal. Our friend and disability warrior, Matt Curcio, put it like this: "I suspect we will find success in interdependence, not independence or codependence."

EMBRACING EXPECTATIONS

1. What is *one thing* you can do this week to build on a relationship within your circle?
2. Check yourself. If you wonder why no one seems to engage with you, examine your attitude and expectations.
3. It's hard to know how much of our story to share, and with whom. If you're one who holds your needs tightly, identify one you could share with someone else. Then do it.

EMBRACING YOUR FRIENDS

1. Nakita Valerio (https://soundtimes.com/we-need-community-care-not-just-self-care/) said, "Shouting 'self-care' at people who actually need 'community care' is how we fail people." What does this mean to you?
2. Reach out to local church friends. Talk with families with disabilities in your community. Is there one thing you can do to serve them better? Remember that, if you build it, they *will* come. Please don't give up, even if we make it hard for you to break into our world. Some days it hurts that much. Persistence will pay off.
3. Gather a small group and read together *Suffering in 3-D* by John Kwasny.

GALATIANS 6:2

"Carry each other's burdens, and in this way you will fulfill the law of Christ."

PRAYER

Lord, you are the true caregiver. None of what is written here shocks you off the throne or is beyond the scope of your care. Help us see our neighbors, disabled and otherwise, as your children in need of your care. But don't allow us to stop there. Please use us to meet those needs. Amen.

FOURTEEN

IS MARRIAGE FOR ME?

Several times a year I hear from someone dating a person with a disability. Jerry and I also meet people with disabilities who see us as a beacon of hope and ask what they can do to get married. Their hope is that maybe somehow, someday, someone will consider dating and marrying them. If this describes you, this is your chapter.

Though we've been married for over a quarter of a century, I remember my single days. Jerry and I met in our late twenties. We were friends for several years before we dated. We got engaged when both of us were thirty-five and were married a year later. During the times before our dates, my friends got married, and I remained alone. Life didn't feel good or fair.

My dad had once commented that I'd never graduate from college with my maiden name, believing that I'd marry by the end of my sophomore year. I think this was because I showed more interest in kids and family life than did my three-years-older sister. She planned to be a missionary and was an accomplished musician.

Dad was right about many things, but not this.

My sister, Ginny, married soon after college. She and her husband served as missionaries in a remote tribal village and raised five children there.

Meanwhile, I yearned to have a husband and family. As the frequent first choice of a babysitter for friends, I gained an inside view of their family dynamics. I learned that, even if I could maneuver a relationship to the point of a wedding, a strong marriage and family wouldn't automatically result. That would require hard work and following God's lead. I surrendered my desires to the Lord and became a contented single person. Then, after I had relinquished my dreams, God fanned into flame my friendship with Jerry.

CONTENTMENT

I don't claim that this is a formula for starting a relationship or for getting married. But contentment[1] with the life with which God had graced us provided the sound foundation on which we could build our relationship.

Contentment undergirds all good relationships, while a life of "what ifs" robs us of present pleasures. Wondering whether every person not wearing a wedding band might be "the one" exhausts us. Understanding that God has our best in mind and loves us with an everlasting love (Jeremiah 31:3) offers security and a safe place to ask questions.

Another building block of contentment is acknowledging that we aren't mistakes, even if we're living with a disability. Psalm 139 describes God knitting each of us together in our mother's womb. I enjoy simple knitting projects. Before I cast the first stitches onto the needle, I have a pattern, or purpose, in mind. For example, I excel at knitting dishcloths. To end with a functional piece, I must use the proper sized needles and purchase yarn of the weight and fibers suitable for washing dishes. Knowing what I want the end product to look like, I knit, purl, increase, or decrease stitches as I move through each row.

God's knitting skill far exceeds mine, yet my experience with needles and yarn helps me understand his care and intention for each of us.

The Bible also tells us that God has a good plan for us. When I use the word "good," don't think of the automatic response we give to the question "How are you today?" Recall instead the most delectable food you've ever tasted, which still frequents your thoughts. Think, *Oh, that was goooooood.*

Yes, God has a goooooood plan for our lives. Part of the way he intentionally knit us in the womb may or may not include marriage. Trusting the One who understands *why* he made us gives us a starting point for each day—whether we are married or single.

Contentment needs to be refreshed regularly. Daily or weekly difficulties offer opportunities to revisit roots of peace and satisfaction—since struggles don't end with marriage vows. Practice now hanging your hope and contentment in Jesus.

LISTING THE IMPORTANT

Females, perhaps more than males, enjoy imagining a future with the person of our dreams. Some even compose, as I did, a list of desirable traits in a future spouse. Part of my list included:

- Loves God more than me.
- Serves God.
- Has a great sense of humor.

- Enjoys travel.
- Will lead me/our family as God directs.

When I was young, I also wanted someone "handsome, a great kisser, tall and athletic." Maturity helped refine my hopes. When I met Jerry, I focused less on his disability and more on who he was. Physical attributes aren't wrong, but they shouldn't carry the same weight as a person's character.

Why is a list important? Hunger for a relationship can allow your emotions to overrule your decision making. Feelings can focus on outer attraction and mask the intentions and heart of another person. A list offers an objective way to evaluate your passion. When you are tempted to focus on how happy you believe someone will make you, a list provides a reality check. Is he/she a person of integrity and spiritual insight who understands self-control? Predetermining your priorities will temper your reactions to the excitement and thrill of the present in light of the rest of your life.

SELF-REFLECTIONS

But you need more than a list; you need to look at yourself. Are *you* a man or woman of similar caliber to the one you are looking for? Consider these questions:

- Are you growing your own character before you give yourself to another?
- Do you know your love language? Do you understand how to speak other love languages?[2]
- Are you a person of integrity?
- Do you know how to lead *and* follow? Do you know when to do each?

- Are you a person of prayer?
- Do you place more importance on your outer or your inner person?

Questions about self-development could fill a book; these are starter prompts. Whether you marry or remain single, developing yourself will make you more attractive in all relationships, from friendship to romance.

As you mature, observe marriages among your friends and family. When you identify a good one, ask how the couple got to that point. What are their tips? When you see a marriage you don't want to emulate, quietly observe and make mental or written notes of what you want to avoid.

After you have a healthy handle on God's plan for you, analyze the way you interact with and accept people. When you're interested in someone, what do you do?

Before you pull out your list (literally or figuratively) and announce, "You're God's plan for me," pray.

The perceived possibility of a relationship is always a right time for prayer. Don't start by requesting that the person ask you out or say yes to your asking for a date. Pray unselfishly *for* that person. Pray for them to know God in a deeper way. Pray for their life circumstances. Pray for their family. Pray for God's blessing and direction in their life. You don't need to tell them you are praying for them. Just do it. While you are at it, remember to pray for yourself in similar ways.

Start, and perhaps stay, as friends. Take part in a small group with that individual. Go to the same events or functions to learn different facets of their personality. I first came to appreciate Jerry's wit and humor when we played Uno with others late into the night. Pursue opportunities to talk. Just talk. Practice being a delightful conversationalist. Learn about that person.

Be sure your closest friends and family members get to know the person, too. Remember that emotional engagement can overrule clear perception. Those who know you best and have loved you dearly for a lifetime may note things you miss, both characteristics or habits calling for concern or caution and positive, encouraging qualities.

You'll thank God for the foundation of friendship if he guides you into love and marriage. If joining your lives isn't the plan, you'll still have a solid friendship to enjoy.

Sometimes marriage is referred to as wedded bliss. It can be bliss. But marriage is also hard. Even the best marriages encounter challenges. Undergirding your relationship with friendship offers the time, commitment, and knowledge to work through hard patches.

THE DISABILITY FACTOR

Two questions inevitably arise. One, when should you talk about the specifics of the disability? And two, how would sex work?

Unless you are meeting and dating solely on a virtual platform or have a hidden disability, the other person already knows something about your disability. The initial friendship before dating lets you each explore and observe how the disability will affect both you and others. Typically, this is a process of gentle revelation; natural conversations will arise. Revealing the more delicate parts of your disability can come when the relationship goes deeper. Consider discussing those details on a need-to-know basis.

If you require an attendant to accompany you on dates, drive, or assist with your feeding and personal care needs, let your date know up front. Explain who the other party is and whether they will be next to you the entire evening, as opposed to across the room or in the car. Share briefly why you need their help. Assume the costs for your attendant's evening to be your responsibility, not your date's.

My answer to the questions about sex may not be popular. I live my life and write based on my understanding of God's Word, the Bible. I believe the intimacy of sex is a gift God gives to those who marry. Between engagement and the wedding, sex is a conversation, not an act, that needs to happen. The lengthier your engagement, the longer you should wait to talk about this. Why? Because when he knit us together, God connected our emotions and pleasure centers. Once we fill our minds with specific details, it becomes harder and harder for us to follow God's standard and wait for marriage.

How does disability impact the act of sex? I'm not skilled or trained to answer that question for you. Even as each person and each disability has different nuances, so does the path of intimacy. Talk with your doctor or ask for a referral to a professional who specializes in this area and seek their counsel and input. If you live in or near a large city, seek out a teaching hospital. Staff members stay up to date on the latest advancements and techniques in all areas of medical care.

Don't get hung up on the act of intercourse. There are many ways for a couple to achieve intimacy, and not all are sexual. As you and your spouse grow in your relationship, you will enjoy exploring together ways that satisfy you both. This is one blessing of marriage.

WISDOM FROM JERRY

Another marriage blessing I enjoy is Jerry's wisdom. I'm delighted to share some of that from a recent interview I did with him:

> Joan: "What would you say to the person with a disability who is single and wants to be married?"
>
> Jerry: "Marriage is a natural desire. God created marriage and put a high value on it. We know that because he uses the marriage metaphor when he calls the Church the bride of Christ. God created singleness, too. At one time, being a single adult meant that you were a mature Christian. I'm not sure that's accurate.
>
> "I'm in favor of marriage. You, Joan, are the only person besides me and God who knows all my mess and still loves me. Marriage offers instantaneous feedback when I look into your face."
>
> Joan: "When you were growing up, do you remember anyone ever talking to you about dating and marriage?"
>
> Jerry: "Not that I recall, although a summer youth camp introduced me to kissing and hormones when I was twelve."
>
> Joan: "Talk about your dating experience."
>
> Jerry: "I could probably count the number of dates I've had on two hands and maybe a foot. I went out with a girl who lived in a nearby town the summer after my freshman year of college. Because she was Catholic, and I was in Bible College, our relationship didn't work

well. In college I dated five or six times but later went for a decade between dates. Looking back, that gap was partly because I didn't know how to approach dating while dealing with my own issues."

Joan: "How did your disability play into the dates you had? Did you have to prepare your date in advance about your disability?"

Jerry: "Not very much. Mine was almost all about emotional issues like Will this person really accept me (when at the same time I couldn't accept me)?

"My experience, and watching friends, taught me that the more you date, the better you get at it. Like anything else, you've got to make time for it. Disability eats up much of my time, so it was difficult. You've got to put the other person at ease with your disability. That adds an extra layer of complexity because you have to figure out if they like you *and* whether the person can deal with your disability."

Joan: "How long does your responsibility to put them at ease last—through the first date or after three dates, or . . . ?"

Jerry: "I rarely got to the third date or even the second. The exception was the person I dated for about six months. She was one of maybe three I thought was 'the one,' but she didn't agree."

Joan: "When a woman didn't want to continue dating, did she ever mention your disability?"

Jerry: "No, but I'm sure that was part of it."

Joan: "You've probably dated a lot more than many other people with disabilities. What about someone who says, 'Wow, Jerry can count up to fifteen dates. I can't even count one, or I can only count one.' What do you say to that person?"

Jerry: "Determine your standards and boundaries. For instance, I was much more legalistic about everything when I was younger, so I practically required my date to attend a church like mine. Figure out your 'must have' list. Be clear about your physical boundaries.

"But most important, you've got to like yourself well enough to picture somebody being with you. And that's difficult. I argue with myself about whether I like myself now, but I'm a lot more comfortable with who I am today than I've ever before been. Work on yourself first.

"Some suggestions apply to all singles; the good news is that you're not essentially much different. You need to go to singles groups and interact while you're there. Introverts, disabled or not, have a harder time. You may start out by just attending. Once you're comfortable, you may talk to an individual or engage during social time.

"In the past, there were dating groups for people with disabilities, one of which existed for nurses who wanted to date people with disabilities. Most of those melded into online dating, which in some ways makes dating easier; technology helps link people, including those with disabilities."

Joan: "You said you thought a few women were 'the one.' Yet you didn't date most of them for a long period. Arriving at the conclusion that they might have been the one seems to have been premature."

Jerry: "Yes, it was."

Joan: "Do you think people can make that determination after one or two dates?"

Jerry: "I think you can decide that someone is a possibility, but that's all. Anecdotal stories say that some people claim to experience love at first sight. While this is possible, normally relationships take time, effort, and practice. Disability makes the process more difficult."

Joan: "What can you do while you're not dating or married to prepare for that time?"

Jerry: "Start saving money. Think about what living on your own looks like. Is it a building on the back of the family property, an apartment nearby, or even buying your own home? Don't expect the person you marry to meet all your needs; no one person can. Consider how you might manage attendant care if you get married. One woman backed off from dating a man with a disability once she realized he wanted her to replace his mother, who had been attending to all his personal care. That's an unfair expectation. Every relationship is unique.

"Figure out how you want to spend your days, whether in a full-time or part-time job or in a volunteer position. Pray about it. Pray specifically."

Joan: "At what point in a relationship would you talk about what's involved in your personal care and how you envision your spouse being involved?"

Jerry: "Probably during our pre-engagement."

Joan: "When you say pre-engagement, can you clarify? Pre-engagement starts on the first date. I think you mean later, when the couple talks about marriage and thinks engagement may be the next step."

Jerry: "Yes. After dating a while—months, maybe even years—once some decisions have been made. The guy is gathering courage to propose. Some choose the anniversary of their first date. Others want the family involved. Some prefer a quiet personal encounter, while others prefer a special event. This is after you've talked about your future and are waiting to decide the details. During that time, discuss personal care. After the engagement, closer to the wedding, start talking about what sex will look like."

Joan: "If someone wonders if or how sex will be possible, given their disability, what would you tell them?"

Jerry: "It is important to have already established your boundaries in advance and agreed to them before you talk. Annually, the February issue of *New Mobility Magazine* focuses on relationships and sexuality for persons with disabilities. This is a broad-based disability magazine. The articles may cover more than you are comfortable with. If you can get past that, you'll find a wealth of resources and frank talk between the covers. There are also books and videos appropriate to this topic."

Joan: "If you're going to have a long engagement of a year or more, would you talk about sex as soon as you've gotten the ring? Or wait till closer to the wedding?"

Jerry: "I'd wait until close to the wedding. Culture leads us to believe that sex is the only part of marriage that matters. That is simply not true."

Joan: "There's something to be said about figuring it out with your beloved after you're married. There are a lot of different techniques and many ways in which the couple can achieve intimacy, both sexually and in ways that don't directly involve intercourse. Part of the fun of marriage is exploring those together."

Jerry: "That's true, but the details and logistical efforts of disability may minimize some of the fun."

Joan: "We don't watch television or movies that are sexually explicit. From what we see in advertisements and on the family-friendly channels, the portrayal of marriage and intimacy is nothing like real life on the first day or weeks after the wedding. Intimacy grows and develops with time."

Jerry: "Agreed. If you go to Hollywood for your education on dating and marriage, you're going to be disappointed, even if you choose the Hallmark® channel.

"You may also want to check out web and print resources specific to your disability."

Joan: "Did anybody ever tell you that, because of your disability, you'd probably never get married? Or that you shouldn't even think about marriage?"

Jerry: "I doubt it. I might not have been listening because I was busy overcoming everything, which is what we're taught to do."

Joan: "We were conference friends for a few years. What changed that made you realize you wanted to take our friendship to a different level?"

Jerry: "I gave God time. I was praying, 'God, I wish there were someone like Joan where I live.' I literally prayed those words. After many weeks, God clearly pointed out that the phone worked from Indiana to California. The more we talked, the more our friendship deepened. Valentine's Day was pivotal. I mean, it was interesting. My secretary knew only that you were sending me a gift, not what it was. She also knew what I planned to send you and told me I needed to up my game, which I did. Apparently it was enough because you're here."

Joan: "The one thing I looked for was whether had you signed the card 'Love, Jerry.' And you hadn't. I thought, *Okay, we're not there yet*. I hadn't signed mine that way, either, because I was waiting for you to make the first move. And just a couple of days later, on Valentine's weekend, you declared your feelings with the now famous words..."

Jerry: "'I think I might be falling in love with you.'

"Immature people and people with disabilities really fear getting hurt. I went out on a limb a little to see what would happen. Risk is okay on some level, but if your overarching purpose is to not get hurt, you're going to miss out on a lot. So, my bottom line is: try it. Pick a step that feels most doable and try."

Joan: "How did you recover when dates told you 'Nope, I don't see this relationship the same way you do'?"

Jerry: "Poorly. That accounts for the long gaps between dates. I didn't want to get hurt anymore. When friends said I was trying too hard, I didn't understand. Now I think I do. Going on a date to have fun—that's a successful date. If you want to go out again, okay. If you ask and the person says, 'I'd love to, but I can't go on Saturday,' you have a choice. You can choose another day or ask someone else. At the casual level, there's nothing wrong with dating multiple people."

Joan: "Any thoughts for the person who needs to take a third party on a date to assist with feeding or personal care?"

Jerry: "In that case, I'd tell my date up front. I might say, 'Joe will help me with my feeding and personal needs' (or whatever it is you'll need). Perhaps your accessible van needs to be driven by someone familiar with it. Make clear what your attendant is there to do and where they will hang out. For example, will the person stay in the van until you text them? Will they sit at a table across the restaurant? Think through your scenarios. Perhaps your date will say, 'If you show me how, I can feed you.' Don't impose the expectation of help on your date without prior discussion."

Joan: "Is there anything else you'd like to share?"

Jerry: "I am so glad I'm married. I'm glad I married you. You really are a picture of God's grace to me. You should put that in the book at least six times."

EMBRACING THE WAIT
1. Don't rush. The payoff is well worth the wait.
2. Learn to hang your satisfaction and contentment on your relationship with God.
3. Clarify your non-negotiables for a spouse. Write them down and commit them to prayer.
4. Establish and practice physical boundaries in your relationships.

EMBRACING YOUR FRIENDS
1. Try to avoid assuming your friend can never marry because of a disability.
2. Pray for them to be prepared for the relationship God may bring, or for their confidence in God's plan if it is for them to remain single.
3. Be lovingly honest about any red flags you observe in your friend's character or in someone they date. Don't hesitate because "They already have enough to deal with being disabled. I don't want to hurt their feelings."

PSALM 139:13-18
"You created my inmost being; you knit me together in my mother's womb. I praise you because I am fearfully and wonderfully made; your works are wonderful, I know that full well. My frame was not hidden from you when I was made in the secret place, when I was woven together in the depths of the earth. Your eyes saw my unformed body; all the days ordained for me were written in your book before one of them came to be. How precious to me are your thoughts, God. How vast is the sum of them. Were I to count them, they would outnumber the grains of sand—when I awake, I am still with you."

PRAYER

Thank you, Creator Father, for the way you knit me together. Please help me be content with your plan and timing. If you have marriage in my future, please continue to mold me and the other person to be more like you. If remaining single is your best plan for me, let me embrace that and enjoy it fully. Amen.

APPENDIX

CINCINNATI CHILI RECIPE (SERVES 8)

This recipe was passed down by my mother-in-law, who found it in a newspaper clipping

- 1 qt water
- 2 medium onions, grated finely
- 1 8 oz can tomato sauce
- 5 whole allspice
- ½ tsp red pepper
- 1 tsp ground cumin seed
- 4 tbsp chili powder
- ½ oz bitter Bakers chocolate
- 2 lbs ground beef
- 4 cloves garlic
- 2 tbsp vinegar
- 1 large bay leaf, whole
- 5 whole cloves
- 2 tsp Worcestershire sauce
- 1½ tsp salt
- 1 tsp cinnamon

Add ground beef to water in a 4 qt pot and stir until beef separates to a fine texture. Boil slowly for half an hour. Add all the other ingredients. Stir to blend, bringing to a boil; reduce heat and simmer uncovered for about 3 hours. Last hour, uncover pot after desired consistency is reached.

Chili may be refrigerated overnight so that fat can be removed before reheating.

Serve over spaghetti noodles and top with dark red kidney beans, diced onions, and finely shredded cheddar cheese. Serve oyster crackers on the side. This is called a five-way.

Another option is to serve it over hot dogs. Spread the hot dog bun with mustard before adding the dog. Top it with chili, diced onions, and cheese.

Whichever way you choose to serve this, enjoy! Send me a picture of yours at Joan@JoanBorton.com.

BUCKEYE RECIPE
Source unknown

Mix together:
- 3 c creamy peanut butter (a 40 oz jar yields 3.5 cups)
- 1½ sticks of softened butter
- 2 lbs powdered sugar

Form into small balls (if needed, refrigerate the mix before shaping). Use a toothpick to dip the balls into melted dipping chocolate (about 1 lb). Dip until almost covered, leaving some of the peanut butter ball exposed on top. Set the buckeye on parchment paper until the chocolate has set.

Refrigerate and enjoy.

I'd love to see your photos when you make these. Send to Joan@ JoanBorton.com.

RESOURCES

Luke 14 Exchange, Inc.
https://luke14exchange.org
Jerry and Joan Borton cofounded Luke 14 Exchange to help bring people affected by disability to God's eternal banquet table. We coach and mentor people affected by disabilities, encourage their family members, and come alongside the ministries that serve them.

Marriage and Caregiving
www.christianneurodiversemarriage.com
Dan and Stephanie Holmes founded the International Association of NeuroDiverse Christian Marriages, LLC to first and foremost bring hope, help, and possible healing to NeuroDiverse Christian Marriages. Their ministry includes educating and equipping helping professionals, clinicians, and ministers in effective coaching and counseling strategies by first understanding and accepting the complexities of neurodiverse Christian marriages.

www.hopeforthecaregiver.com
Peter Rosenberger has long been a voice for family caregivers. He has journeyed through more than eighty-five surgeries for his wife, Gracie, and knows first-hand what it means to be a caregiving spouse. Connect with Peter through his private Facebook group, podcast, music, and books.

https://theheartofthecaregiver.com
Mary Tutterow is a wife, mom, author, speaker, teacher, and caregiver. She states, "I wrote *The Heart of the Caregiver*® during some of our most difficult years. It is now my joy to help other frazzled caregivers find beautiful transformation in the caregiving process—for themselves, their family, and the people they care for."

Disability Related Travel (please note that not all of these resources are faith-based.)

https://accessiblego.com
The first-ever accessible hotel booking site.

https://wheelchairtravel.org
Loaded with information on domestic and international destinations for travelers with disabilities.

www.luke5adventures.org
For those who aren't physically able to hike it, forge it, climb it, cross it, or ascend it, Luke 5 Adventures makes it possible.

ACKNOWLEDGMENTS

We were married for only a few short years when I said, "Someone needs to write a marriage book about how to lead while sitting and submit while standing." I was struggling with how to embrace the many nuances of a marriage affected by disability. My husband, Jerry, replied, "That someone is you." As the years progressed, his words took on greater urgency: "Write the book." Without his encouragement, love, prayers, and nearly nightly foot rubs, this book would remain only in my head. Thank you, Jerry, for lovingly prodding me. And for your humor and willingness to let me share dozens of our stories.

The wedding day is the focal point for many couples. For us, the ceremony was the start of applying the excellent premarital counsel we had received from our then pastor, Rich Cundall. Thank you. We'll never forget the top ten (or was it twenty?) lists you had us create and how Jerry put the final amen on your prayer of consecration when his vest button flew off. And, by the way, Jerry still hasn't shown me that paper you gave him, marked "for husbands only."

While Jerry's encouragement motivated me, my good friends from Word Weavers International continue to teach me how to write. Through conferences, critique groups, and friendships built with other writers, my skills have improved. Word Weavers calls face-to-face groups chapters identified by location. The online groups are known as Pages, identified with a number. My deepest thanks go to the writers I've met through Pages 13, 29, and 42. After we moved to Florida, the Tampa chapter of Word Weavers welcomed me to face-to-face meetings. The other participants were nothing but gracious and encouraging as I bared my soul for them to read and refine my efforts through their critiques. Thank you for loving me and the concept of this book enough to make both better.

Out of Word Weavers, some individuals made time to invest in me on a one-on-one basis. I am much obliged to Tez Brooks, Britt Mooney, Lyneta Smith, Kathy Thomas, Carol Pierce, and Jan Powell.

I am grateful for Anne Adams, Marianne Charles, and Hannah Huber, who prayed me through the years of writing.

To the board and team at Luke 14 Exchange, Inc., I am indebted. You not only allowed me time to write but took other things off my plate so that I've had little else to focus on but the book for these last several months. Thank you for believing in me and in the need for this book.

Thank you to the couples who allowed me to interview you and use part of your stories in the following chapters. I value your honesty. To protect it, I identified each couple with pseudonyms.

Many men from our churches in Pennsylvania and Florida committed to handling Jerry's personal care for a long weekend every quarter. These breaks allowed me an uninterrupted period to write. Sometimes I went to a hotel. At other times friends hosted me, knowing that I wouldn't be social while there. What a gift each of you gave to me.

And, finally, thank you to my beta readers. I felt vulnerable when I sent you the draft of the manuscript and asked for your honest feedback. You were gentle and kind, even as your thoughts sharpened me. I appreciate you more than words can tell.

ENDNOTES

1. www.crosswalk.com/family/marriage/relationships/what-it-i-really-i-means-when-two-become-one.html.
2. www.nytimes.com/1999/05/31/us/disabled-spouses-are-increasingly-forced-to-go-it-alone.html#:~:text=Louis%20Harris%20%26%20Associates%2C%20which%20has,and%209%20percent%20in%201984.
3. Genesis 2:34; Ephesians 5:25–33; Mark 10:8; Matthew 19:5–6; 1 Corinthians 6:16.
4. Peter Rosenberger, Hope for the Caregiver (Brentwood, TN: Worthy Inspired), 2014.
5. www.bryanstoudt.com/god-really-want-women-submit.
6. www.researchgate.net/publication/23685321_Intimate_Relationships_and_Women_Involved_in_the_Sex_Trade_Perceptions_and_Experiences_of_Inclusion_and_Exclusion.
7. www.dictionary.com/browse/intimacy.
8. www.mentalhelp.net/blogs/the-most-important-tool-for-restoring-emotional-intimacy-to-your-marriage/.
9. www.desiringgod.org/articles/six-ways-to-pursue-spiritual-intimacy-in-marriage.

10. For more on intimacy and dementia, read: https://teepasnow.com/blog/how-to-discuss-sexuality-and-intimacy-2-0/.
11. www.guinnessworldrecords.com/news/2015/2/valentines-day-ten-of-the-most-romantic-world-records-371925.
12. www.yourtango.com/201187899/some-married-couples-kiss-only-once-week.
13. www.marriageandfamilytoday.com/10-second-kiss-challenge/.
14. https://caregiver.com/articles/caregiver-stress-syndrome/.
15. http://edition.cnn.com/2007/HEALTH/conditions/08/13/caregiver.syndrome/index.html#:~:text=Many%20exhausted%2C%20ill%20caregivers%20today,are%20depression%2C%20anxiety%20and%20anger.
16. http://edition.cnn.com/2007/HEALTH/conditions/08/13/caregiver.syndrome/index.html.
17. See resources in the appendix.
18. www.merriam-webster.com/words-at-play/what-does-macgyver-mean-slang-definition.
19. www.epm.org/blog/2016/Jun/10/robertson-mcquilkin.
20. www.goodreads.com/quotes/71023-grow-old-along-with-me-the-best-is-yet-to#:~:text=Join%20Goodreads&text=in%20with%20Facebook-,Grow%20old%20along%20with%20me!,See%20all%2C%20nor%20be%20afraid!

www.ingramcontent.com/pod-product-compliance
Lightning Source LLC
Chambersburg PA
CBHW070146100426
42743CB00013B/2830